Collins Revision

KS3

English

Revision Guide

Levels 6-7

Kim Richardson

Revision Guide Contents

Workbook Contents

About Key Stage 3 English

This book has been written to help you practise the necessary skills to raise your level in Key Stage 3 English. It gives you lots of practice texts to analyse, different types of questions to try and helpful tips and hints on how to improve. It will give you the confidence to make good progress at KS3 and then GCSE.

What does Key Stage 3 English involve?

- KS3 English is split into three skill areas: reading, writing and speaking and listening (speaking and listening is counted as one).

Reading

- You will have lessons and assessments that focus on how well you read for meaning and look beyond the surface of a text. This means you have to consider how the text is written, why it is written and the impact it has on the reader.

- There are lots of activities and support in this book to help you develop your reading skills.

Writing

- During KS3 English you will also spend lots of time planning and writing a wide variety of texts. Your work reading texts will help you understand how to construct effective texts yourself.

- These texts will cover lots of different purposes such as writing to argue, describe and even review.

- Once again, we've included plenty of activities to support you as you learn to develop these skills.

Speaking and listening

- Don't forget this really important part of English! As you learn about Reading and Writing you'll also develop your Speaking and Listening skills – essential if you are to communicate effectively in all situations.

- Try explaining your ideas about the activities and texts in this book to someone – this is a great way to develop your confidence and clarity of style.

And finally... literature

- As well as English, you'll also study Literature at school, most often in the same lesson. Poetry, prose and drama written by others are a great way to develop your key English skills.

- You'll study various authors, from pre-1914 to modern day, but the most famous one has to be Shakespeare!

- You have to study at least one of Shakespeare's plays in KS3 and another in KS4, so it's good to get as much practice as possible now. This book contains all you need to impress your teacher and classmates as you start to study 'The Bard'.

Top Tip!

The more you read, the more your English skills will improve.

Different text types

- Throughout your Key Stage 3 course, you will read a variety of texts and will be assessed on how you evaluate the pieces of writing and how you answer questions on them.

- Your teacher may give you different texts to compare, sometimes on the same **theme** (e.g. animals, communication or time travel), but they will be written in different **styles**.

- They will normally be a combination of fiction and non-fiction texts. The non-fiction texts will be in different **forms**, e.g. book extract, newspaper report, interview, leaflet, diary, advert … all sorts.

- The texts will have different **purposes**, e.g. to explain, to tell a story, to persuade an audience, to review a film.

Pages 8, 12, 16, 20, 24 (different types of text).

How to read a text

- When you are practising your comprehension skills, make sure you take your time to read the extract carefully.

- As you read, you can highlight or underline any **key words or phrases**. Also, try to notice **key features** of the texts, such as their structure, how language is used and the mood or tone of the writing.

Pages 10, 14, 18, 22, 26 (key features).

- You don't need to remember everything in the texts. You will be able to re-read the important bits when you answer the questions.

Different question types

- In practice tests, some questions may be short, and only give you 1 mark each. Others will be longer, and may give you up to 5 marks.

- You may be asked to write a word, a sentence or a paragraph. You may be asked to tick a box, fill in a table or complete a sentence.

- The questions may ask you to:
  - **find information**
  - **comment** on language or structure
  - give your **opinion**
  - **explain** the writer's **viewpoint and purpose**.

Pages 28–37 (answering different types of question).

Answering the questions

- Start at the beginning and work your way through the questions. The first few questions refer to the first text, and so on.

- **Do exactly what you are asked.** If you are asked to write a word or phrase, don't write an essay.

- Look at the **marks** given for each question. They will give you an idea about how much you should write.

- When commenting or explaining, **refer closely to the text** in your answer.

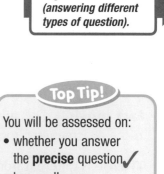

Top Tip!

You will be assessed on:
- whether you answer the **precise** question ✓
- how well you understand the texts ✓
- how well you comment on their language, structure and purpose ✓

You will *not* be assessed on:
- your writing style ✗
- your spelling, punctuation or grammar ✗

Good practice

- When doing practice tests, use the **marks** as a guide. You shouldn't spend more than 2 minutes per mark.

- Leave 5 minutes at the end to **read through and check** your answers.

Spot Check

Look at these questions. What type of answer is each question asking for? **a** explaining the writer's viewpoint, **b** giving your opinion, **c** commenting on language, **d** finding information

1 Which words show that Sam is frightened?
2 Comment on the writer's use of language to describe how frightened Sam is.
3 Explain how the writer structures the passage to show Sam's fear gradually increasing.
4 What do you think Sam is most frightened of in this passage?

What is fiction?

- Fiction means **stories** which describe imaginary events in a way that entertains the reader. The text on the page opposite is the opening to a novel.

- Some stories have a **message** or **moral**, for example fables or religious stories.

- The key features of a story to comment on are the **plot**, **language**, **setting** and **characters**.

Pages 10–11 (characters).

Plot

- The plot is the **storyline**. Plots often have a similar structure – an introduction, a development (build up), a crisis and a resolution (when things are sorted out).

- **Fast moving** plots are exciting and full of tension. **Slow moving** plots focus more on character, mood and description.

- **Theme** is different from **plot**. Themes are the underlying ideas or issues that the story deals with. For example, the plot of *Private Peaceful* follows the fortunes of two soldiers in World War I. Its **themes** include growing up, bravery, bullying and war.

Language

- Words are chosen carefully to create a precise effect. Writers use **descriptive detail** and **imagery**, as in this extract from the text opposite: *for a moment the page of the London A to Z he was supposed to be reading blurred and swam beneath his eyes.*

- Writers pay attention to the **structure** of their sentences and how they **sound**, e.g. *Quickly he knuckled the wet from his face. Had his mother noticed? If she had, he would say it was sweat. And that he felt sick.*

Setting

- The setting is the **place** and **time** in which the story is set.

- The way the author describes the setting contributes to the **mood** or **atmosphere** of the story. You can see an example in the opening of the extract opposite, which is set in a hot, smelly meat market.

Top Tip!

To get a higher level you need to be able to comment on **how** the setting of a story helps create a particular atmosphere or mood.

Spot Check

1 What are the four key features of stories?
2 Explain what the resolution of a story is.
3 Think about a novel or short story you have read. What is the plot? What are the themes?

This is the opening passage from a novel.

How does the author make the reader want to read on?

> It was the stench seeping in through the car windows that bothered Tom the most. Rank and beefy, it reminded him of the way dogs smell after a walk in the rain. Smelly dogs made him think of Goldie, left behind in Dorset, and for a moment the page of the London *A to Z* he was supposed to be reading blurred and swam beneath his eyes.
>
> Quickly he knuckled the wet from his face. Had his mother noticed? If she had, he would say it was sweat. And that he felt sick. It was late morning, the middle of August, and hot enough for even a skinny twelve year old to be melting like a lolly. Add the stink of Smithfield meat market, leaching through traffic fumes, and anyone with nostrils and a stomach in working order was bound to feel bad.

(From *Follow Me Down*, by Julie Hearn)

level
7

Answer

The author tells us just enough so that we can make sense of what is going on, but leaves lots of questions unanswered for the moment. For example, the boy seems to be in a car going through London, and there's a horrible smell from the meat market. But we don't know why he is there, and why the thought of his dog makes his eyes fill with tears.

The language is vivid and powerful, for example the words 'stench' and 'rank and beefy' to describe the smell. The good description draws us in to the story.

Also, we are told straight away what the main character thinks and feels, so we identify with him. The story is 'alive' from the start.

Did You Know?

The author John Creasey wrote 565 books in 40 years. Twenty-six of them were written in a single year!

Characters

- **Believable** and **interesting** characters are central to the success of a story.

- Things happen to characters, but characters also **develop** (change) through a story.

- Characters affect each other. These **relationships** are often the key aspects of a story.

- **Characterisation** means how an author presents and develops their characters.

Describing characters

You can learn about characters in different ways:

- by **how they look**, e.g. *He had small piercing eyes that were set too closely together.*

- by **how they speak**, e.g. *"Found a shilling, huh?" His voice was gruff. "Want to show me?"*

- by **what they do**, e.g. *He sidled up to me, then grabbed at my hand and sank his teeth into it.*

- by **what others say and do**, e.g. *Harriet let out a shriek of laughter. "You really are desp'rate, en't ya?" she said.*

> **Top Tip!**
> To get a level 6 you'll need to be able to give your **own impression** of a character, not just describe what they are like.

Dialogue

- Characters' speech is called **dialogue**.

- Dialogue can include different **accents** (pronunciatic and **dialect** (e.g. regional versions of speech).

- Each character will have their own way of speaking, which will be **consistent** through the story.

Narrative viewpoint

- The point of view from which the story is told is called the **narrative viewpoint**.

- A **1st person narrative** is written as if one of the characters is telling it, e.g. *I opened the package carefully.*

- A **3rd person narrative** is told by the author, e.g. *Nasreem opened the package carefully.*

- A **3rd person narrative** is often written from the point of view of one of the characters. The extract on page 9 is written from Tom's point of view.

Read the extract on page 9 again.

(a) What impressions do you get of Tom's state of mind?
(b) How does the narrative voice affect how we feel about Tom?

Answer

(a) Tom is a bit agitated. He is bothered most of all by the smell of the meat market (first sentence), but this makes him think about his dog. This makes his eyes fill with tears (the page 'blurred and swam'), so he is sad.

But he doesn't want his mother to see that he is sad – he is prepared to 'say it was sweat'. Although he is very hot and feeling sick from the smell, this is all he wants his mother to know about what is wrong.

(b) This is a third person narrative, but it is written very much from Tom's viewpoint. We are 'under his skin' and feeling and seeing (and smelling) with him. That makes us want to know even more what he is doing in London and why he is sad.

level 7

Comment

This is a level 7 answer because it shows understanding of all of Tom's feelings. The analysis of the narrative viewpoint is accurate and well written. The student gives a personal response to the text and supports the points made by detailed and relevant reference to the text.

Did You Know?

The evil Professor Snape in the Harry Potter books is supposed to be based on the head of science who taught the author, J K Rowling.

Spot Check

Choose a story you have read recently.
1 Who is the main character(s)?
2 How does he or she (or they) develop through the story?
3 What narrative viewpoint has the author chosen?

Reading texts that persuade, argue, advise

Purpose and audience

Some texts try to get the reader to do something, e.g. buy a product, agree with the writer's point of view or act in a certain way. For example:

- Adverts try to **persuade** you to buy an iPod or travel to Portugal.

- Newspaper articles or editorials **argue** that footballers get paid too much, or that we should recycle more.

- Health leaflets and magazine articles may **advise** you on how to eat or exercise properly.

> **Top Tip!**
>
> When commenting on an extract, remember to think about:
> - its **purpose** – why it has been written
> - the **audience** – who it is aimed at.

Structure

- The writing is usually presented as a series of points in a **logical order**.

- **Topic sentences** often introduce each point.

- **Connectives** show the reader how the ideas are connected, e.g. *however, another point is …, in addition, on the other hand*.

- A powerful **opening** grabs the reader's attention, and a good **ending** has a lasting effect.

Rhetorical techniques

Rhetorical techniques are used to help get the message across effectively. They include:

- **Repetition**, e.g. *Let there be justice for all. Let there be peace for all.*

- Using **personal pronouns** – 'you' addresses the audience directly; 'we' includes the audience on the writer's side.

- **Rhetorical questions**, e.g. *Are we going to give up?* or *Isn't it better that …?*

- **Sound effects**, e.g. alliteration (*nuisance neighbours*) and rhyme (*a bad law, not a mad law*).

- **Emotive language** – language designed to make the audience feel something strongly, e.g. *They are destroying children's lives.*

Design and layout

Adverts and leaflets have **visual appeal**. This makes them attractive and easy to read. Here are some features to comment on:

- **Pictures** In an advert, the picture may be more important than the text.

- **Columns** The text is often in columns to make it easy to read.

- **Design** Colour, font style and size, use of bold/italic, use of space, graphics – all play a part in getting the message across.

- **Subheadings** They break up the text into manageable sections and guide the reader.

Examples

> **Worried about getting spots? The best thing is to eat a healthy balanced diet. It's not too difficult – you just need to:**
> - *have at least 5 portions of fruit and veg every day*
> - *eat starchy foods, such as potatoes and rice*
> - *go easy on the dairy products, such as cheese and milk.*

A typical advice text. Note the conversational tone, direct address to reader, and bullet point list.

Did You Know?

The first advert on TV was for Gibbs toothpaste, in 1955. The slogan was, "It's tingling fresh. It's fresh as ice. It's Gibbs SR toothpaste."

> Text messaging is destroying conversation. Have you noticed how people spend the whole time with their noses in their keypads? Not only that, it is wrecking children's spelling and grammar. We should push up the price of texting before standards slip any further.

A typical argument text. Note the clear points made, with reasons, and the rhetorical question.

A typical advert. Note the appealing image, attractive design and clever slogan.

Spot Check

1 What is the purpose of an advert? Give three ways in which adverts achieve their purpose.
2 What does the connective 'however' signal in a piece of writing?
3 Why do texts that persuade, argue or advise often begin with a question?

Fact

- A **fact** is something that **can be proved** to be true:
  Peter Jackson's film 'King Kong' was made in 2005.
  If people don't agree, you can check facts and show them the evidence.

- An opinion is someone's **point of view**:
  'King Kong' was a fabulous film.
  This cannot be proved to be true. It is someone's personal judgement on the film.

Where you find opinions

You need to look out for **opinions** in all sorts of writing, e.g.

- **reviews** – where the reviewer gives their opinion about a film, CD or book

- **adverts** – where the audience is persuaded to agree with an opinion about a product

- **newspaper** and **magazine articles**, which argue for or against an opinion.

Persuasive opinions

Opinions can be very persuasive:

- They can **disguise themselves as facts**, e.g. *Everyone knows that …*

- They can use **powerful words**, especially adjectives, e.g. *a perfect gift for Christmas*

- They can use **emotive language** e.g. *the holiday of your dreams* or *These men are preying on our children*.

Bias

Writers show **bias** when their language presents an **unfair picture** of something.

- They could **pretend** something is a fact, or **exaggerate** facts or **select** facts in an unfair way.

- They could use a lot of emotive language to **manipulate** our feelings.

Read this extract from a Greenpeace advert.

How does the writer use language to persuade the reader to help the campaign?

> 'staggering' is the writer's opinion. It's a strong word.

> 'ancient' is a powerful adjective that makes us want to preserve the forests.

> 'pristine' (untouched) is a powerful adjective that makes us want to keep our hands off them.

Protecting ancient forests

A staggering 80% of the world's ancient forests have already been destroyed or degraded. Each year, millions of hectares of ancient forests are logged, often illegally, driven by international demand for cheap timber and other wood products, including paper. The UK is Europe's worst offender, with up to 50% of our tropical plywood coming from Indonesia's pristine rainforests. In Indonesia, an estimated 80% of the orang-utan's natural habitats have been wiped out in the last 20 years.

LOVE

> Facts are given in the form of figures, though 'up to 50%' is a bit vague.

> The reference to orang-utan being 'wiped out' is emotive language. The word LOVE in the photo is also emotive.

Top Tip!

- To gain average marks you must **show the techniques** a writer has used to persuade the audience.
- To gain top marks you need to **explain how the writer has used** those techniques.

Did You Know?

It has been estimated that there are over a million words in the English language – over two million if all scientific terms are included.

Spot Check

1 Are these facts or opinions?
  a It makes no difference if you skip breakfast.
  b Some people eat eggs and bacon for breakfast.
2 Explain how these newspaper headlines about GM food are biased.

FRANKENSTEIN FOODS   *FOOD TO FEED OUR FUTURE*

Reading texts that inform and recount

INFORMATION

Look out for these key features:

Purpose and audience

- **Information** texts include reference books, travel guides and leaflets.

- Their **purpose** is to give information about people, places and things.

- The **audience** is people who want to find out about something.

Structure

- Clear **organisation** and **logical order** of topics. **Subheadings** and other **presentational devices** guide reader.

- **General statements** or **main points** first, then examples.

- **Tables** and **diagrams** might add information.

Language

- **Present tense** and **3rd person** (*he, she, it*) used, unless it is information about the past.

- Clear, concise sentences.

- Usually **formal** English, and can include specialist words.

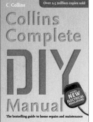

Top Tip!

If you are asked to comment on the layout of an information leaflet, think about the images, colours, font style and size, as well as how the images and writing work together.

RECOUNT

Look out for these key features:

Purpose and audience

- **Recount** texts include newspaper reports, travel writing and biography.

- Their **purpose** is to retell events.

- Their **audience** is people who want to find out what happened, and often to be entertained.

Structure

- Events are told in **chronological order**.

- **Time connectives** guide the reader, e.g. *then* or *the following day*.

- New **paragraphs** mark a change of focus, such as a new time, place or person.

Language

- **Past tense**, though present tense can be used in newspaper stories.

- **Descriptive language** to bring events to life, e.g. adjectives, powerful verbs, imagery.

Page 18.

- Specific **details** given – dates, times, names, descriptions, etc.

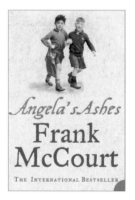

Articles in popular newspapers give information in a particular way:

Catchy **headline** in full caps draws reader in.

DEATH OF THE LADETTE

Old-fashioned girls don't want to party

Subheading tells you more about the subject of the article.

By-line gives reporter's name.

1st paragraph sums up the story. Note bold font.

Next few paragraphs give **more detail**.

Each **paragraph** is only one sentence. More serious papers have slightly longer paragraphs.

Source of article given – a new survey.

Subheading used to catch eye and break up text. Picks up a word from the text.

Quotations from survey given in inverted commas.

Photos and **layout** more important in popular newspaper stories than in serious newspapers.

■ by LAURA NEILL

BRITISH women are rejecting the ladette lifestyle for an old-fashioned family role.

They're turning their backs on the hard partying made famous by the likes of Sarah Cox, 31, and Zoe Ball, 34.

Instead the so-called 'new traditionalists' are married with children.

And they put the family before money and career, though they can combine both.

The new generation of 25 to 45-year-olds has been identified in a new survey.

They admire the values of their mother's era and believe in cooking and knitting, which has become trendy with the stars.

Twist

They snub food fads but know enough about health issues to realise what they should and shouldn't eat, according to the study for drinks firm Ovaltine.

Interviews with 500 women in the 25-45 age group found many wanted life to be 'more like the old days' with a modern twist.

Did You Know?

The book ...*All That Men Know About Women*, which was published in 1996, has 200 pages – but they're all blank!

Spot Check

1 What is the difference between a biography and an autobiography?
2 Would you expect diaries to be written in the 1st or 3rd person?
3 'News stories in popular newspapers aim to entertain as well as inform.' True or false?

Using the senses

- The senses are: looking, hearing, smelling, tasting and feeling. A good writer will make you use your senses:

  I felt my legs buckle beneath me. The ground rose up and hit me between my eyes. The earth didn't taste too good.

- A **visual image** is particularly important, as it lets the reader 'see' what is happening.

Imagery

Look out for these special ways of creating an image, or picture:

- **similes**, which compare something to something else, e.g. *Each harsh word was like the lash of a whip.*

- **metaphors**, which describe something as something else, e.g. *His body was a finely tuned machine which needed constant maintenance.*

- **personification**, which describes non-human things as if they were people, e.g. *The wind provided a helping hand as he cycled up the final hill.*

Top Tip!

Remember that a **simile** uses the words 'like' or 'as' to compare two things. A **metaphor** describes something directly as another thing.

Other descriptive devices

- **Powerful words**, especially adjectives and verbs, e.g. *The eagle plummeted into the bleak landscape.*

- **Alliteration**, e.g. *Defeated and disgraced, he stepped out of the ring.*

- **Detail and elaboration,** which adds weight to a description and makes it vivid.

- **Varied sentences** – using sentences of different lengths and types.

Spot Check

1 What kind of imagery are the following:
   a On the morning of my exam the sun rose reluctantly.
   b The flames of her hair crackled as she tossed her head.
   c He used his pen like a sword to attack his critics.
2 Explain how each one is an effective description.

Question

Read this email, which Ellen MacArthur sent on day 21 of her record-breaking voyage round the world.

What makes her description of the storm effective?

New Message

| Send | New | Attach | Find | Font | Print |

To:

Subject:

Last night was a dark night, hard to see anything out there – nothing but the constant noise of B&Q[1] speeding through the water, the howling wind and the breaking of the waves. The waves are so steep here that poor B&Q feels like she's either running down a hill or being pushed hard up one. Waves regularly break on the windward float quarter. What is noticeable through the dark, shining brighter than our glowing instruments, are the crests of phosphorescence[2] – unbelievable, beautiful, and at times immense. We spend our time, even when trying to rest huddled in a ball in the cuddy[3], just feeling where we are on each mountain, how fast, how far and when will we hit the bottom …

[1]Ellen's boat
[2]tiny sea creatures that glow in the dark
[3]small sheltered area on board

Answer

It is a good description because Ellen uses <u>senses</u>. She makes us see things (the dark, then the glowing creatures) and hear things (the howling wind and breaking waves). She also tells us what she feels like in the last sentence.

level 7

She describes the waves as hills, and later on as mountains. This is an effective <u>metaphor</u> as it makes us see how steep they are.

There are some <u>powerful words</u>, such as the three adjectives used to describe the sea creatures, and 'huddled' up asleep.

Finally, Ellen gives some <u>detail</u> about the boat – where the waves break exactly – which makes us picture the scene.

INSTRUCTION

Look out for these key features:

Purpose and audience

- **Instruction** texts include recipes, directions and DIY manuals.

- Their **purpose** is to tell you how to do something in a series of sequenced steps.

- The **audience** is someone who wants to know how to do that thing.

Structure

- A series of step-by-step instructions in **chronological order**.

- May begin with a **list** of materials/ingredients needed.

- **Layout** makes the instructions easy to follow. May include diagrams, a numbered list, etc.

Language

- Uses **present tense**, **direct address** (you…) and **commands**, e.g. *Break six eggs into a bowl.*

- Written in **simple**, **clear sentences**, in formal English.

- Paragraphs are **short**.

- Includes **time connectives**, e.g. *first* or *then*.

EXPLANATION

Look out for these key features:

Purpose and audience

- **Explanation** texts include encyclopedias, science textbooks and letters explaining absence from school.

- Their **purpose** is to help someone understand how or why something happens, or how to do something.

- The **audience** is someone who wants find out how something works, or how to do something.

Structure

- A series of **logical steps**.

- Each new point has a **new paragraph**. **Topic sentences** may introduce each paragraph.

- **Diagrams** or **illustrations** may help help the verbal explanation.

Language

- **Present tense**, though past tense is used if explaining historical events.

- **Causal connectives** to guide the reader, e.g. *because* or *as a result*. Also **connectives of time**, e.g. *next*.

- **Formal language**, e.g. *An electric current is generated by special muscle cells in the fish* (note the **passive**). **Specialist** or **technical terms** may be used.

> **Page 26 (formal language).**

Top Tip!

To gain a level 7 you need to be able to say not just why a text has been written (its **purpose**), but also **how successful** the writer is in achieving that purpose.

Note how this text both instructs and explains.

Opening is written in amusing way, to draw the reader in. Explanation texts can be entertaining.

Note **connectives** 'so' (causal) and 'once' (time).

Formal language – note technical terms.

How to teach a child to ride a bike
"Of course I won't let go," fibs even the most doting dad, puffing away madly as he runs behind his child's bike. A moment later he takes his hand away …

There is a better way. Children are instinctively able to 'scoot', so get them used to the bike by scooting first. Once they grow out of riding with stabilisers, remove the bike's pedals, then lower the seat so your child can sit with both feet comfortably on the ground.

Now they can scoot along using both feet. This way they learn how to balance and turn on two wheels without also having to cope with the destabilising circular motion of the pedals.

Clear description of the **purpose** of the writing.

New point, so **new paragraph**. Note topic sentence.

Imperatives (remove, lower) and **direct address** (your child).

Sequence of points in chronological order.

(Adapted from *Dad Stuff*, by Steve Caplin and Simon Rose)

Did You Know?

The first English cookbook, 'Forme of Cury', was written in 1390 by the cooks of Richard II. These weren't curry recipes – 'cury' was the Old English word for 'cooking'!

Spot Check

1 What kind of text are the rules of the card game Racing Demon?
2 What is an imperative?
3 When is it useful to use the passive? Give an example.

Putting texts together

Structure refers to the way in which a text or passage is put together. This depends on its **purpose**:

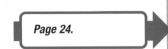

Page 24.

- An **instruction** text is made up of a clear sequence of steps.

- A discussion (or **discursive**) text may begin with a general introduction, then explore each point of view in turn, then conclude.

- An **argument** text may begin with the key point of view, then give reasons and evidence, then conclude.

- A **narrative** text may have an introduction, a development, a crisis and a resolution.

What makes a good structure?

- The points are **well organised** – in chronological order (e.g. for instructions) or with the main points first.

- A new **paragraph** is used for each new point or topic.

- Paragraphs may begin with a **topic sentence**, or a general point, and continue with the detail.

- **Connectives** show how the ideas are linked, and where the ideas are going, e.g. *in addition* or *next*.

From start to finish

Structure also refers to the way in which a text begins and ends. This also depends on the purpose of the text.

- The **beginning** may introduce a topic, or draw the reader in with some powerful language or ideas.

- The **end** may sum up the passage (a conclusion), or have a surprising twist, or neatly refer back to the beginning in some way.

Spot Check

1 How do connectives help the structure of a passage?
2 In which of these texts would you find topic sentences?
   Recipe, Novel, Information leaflet, History essay
3 How could the end of a passage refer back to the beginning?

Narrative structure

- **Plots** often have this structure – an introduction, a development (build up), a crisis and a resolution (when things are sorted out).

- You may be asked how **effective** the beginning of a story is, or how well the author **builds up the tension** in a passage.

Top Tip!

To gain a level 7 you may need to do more than identify **how** a writer has structured a passage. You may also have to say **how successful** she or he has been.

Question

Re-read 'How to teach a child to ride a bike' on page 21.

How well has the author structured the text to achieve his purpose?

Answer

The passage is an instruction text (with a bit of explanation as well), so the author has made sure that it is organised very logically. He begins by showing you how it isn't done, then he takes you through the steps needed to do it properly.

There is a new paragraph for each point, and the ideas in the sentences are sometimes linked by connectives, such as 'first' and 'then'. This makes the explanation easy to understand.

The opening paragraph is unusual, because it is funny, but it is effective as it makes you laugh and want to read on. The end isn't as successful – there's a very long sentence which is hard to follow.

level 7

Comment

This is a level 7 answer. It covers all the aspects of structure – overall organisation of material, paragraphing and connectives, and the purpose of the opening and ending. It also gives a personal response – the student isn't afraid to criticise the effectiveness of the ending. The short quotations from the text are appropriate.

Did You Know?

In his novel *The French Lieutenant's Woman* (1969), the author John Fowles gives the reader a choice of two endings – a happy one or a sad one.

DISCUSSION TEXTS

Look out for these key features:

Purpose and audience

- **Discussion** (or discursive) texts include in-depth newspaper articles on important issues and student essays in RE or History.

- Their **purpose** is to analyse an issue, exploring different points of view.

- They differ from argument texts because they present a **balanced view**.

Structure

- An **introduction** states the issue to be discussed.

- Each **view**, or point, is explored in turn.

- **Connectives** show the reader how the ideas are connected, e.g. *however, another point is …, on the other hand.*

- A **conclusion** may summarise the arguments or give a personal view.

Language

- **Present tense** and **3rd person** (*he, she, it*), e.g. *Some evidence suggests …*

- **Formal** language and a **restrained tone** – the arguments are presented fairly.

> **Top Tip!**
>
> Most discussion texts are serious – look out for **formal** language. Most reviews are lighter in tone – look out for **informal** language.

REVIEWS

Look out for these key features:

Purpose and audience

- A **review** is a way of **giving an opinion** about a book, play, film, etc.

- It is meant to **inform** the reader, and **persuade** them to buy/read/watch the work (or not!).

- The **audience** of reviews want to find out about the work, and sometimes to be entertained.

Structure

- It often begins with some basic **information** about the work.

- A series of **paragraphs** covers different points, e.g. a book review may cover plot, characters, setting and style.

- A **conclusion** may sum up the reviewer's opinion.

Language

- **Present tense** with **3rd person** when describing the work, e.g. *The film is fabulous.*

- Sentences packed with **detail**, e.g. *It mixes rip-roaring action writing with high-tech funk.*

- Often a **friendly** and **informal tone** to get on the reader's side, e.g. *What a yawn of a book.*

Note the features of this discussion text:

Short **introduction** to the issue.

1st viewpoint. 'Most religious people' signals who hold this view.

2nd viewpoint. 'Supporters of euthanasia' signals who hold this view.

Should euthanasia be legalised?

Euthanasia means deliberately bringing a peaceful death to someone who wants it – they may be terminally ill or in great pain. It is a highly controversial issue.

Most religious people say that only God can give and take away life. These people cannot agree with assisted dying or suicide. Opponents of voluntary euthanasia also say that it is a slippery slope to a situation where the sick or elderly will be killed against their will.

Supporters of euthanasia, however, point out that it is based on the right to choose your own death, which is very different from murder. Furthermore, there are some religious people who support euthanasia, especially in the Netherlands.

For myself, I wouldn't want to live in terrible pain, so I think euthanasia should be legalised.

Title raises the question to be discussed.

Connectives show how ideas are connected.

Conclusion here gives a personal view.

The views are presented **fairly** and in **formal** language.

Did You Know?

Paperback books were not produced until 1935. They were an instant success, bringing books to a much wider audience.

Spot Check

1 Are discussion texts usually biased?
2 When would you use the phrase 'on the other hand' in a discussion text?
3 Why would you read a CD review?
4 If a review covers plot, direction, acting and special effects, what is it reviewing?

Tone

- Tone refers to the **mood** or **style** of a piece of writing, e.g. a light-hearted tone, a serious tone or an angry tone.

- The tone a writer chooses depends on the **purpose** and **audience** of the writing. For example, an advice leaflet aimed at teenagers will have a more conversational tone than a news report in a serious newspaper.

Top Tip!

To help you identify tone, imagine you are reading the piece of writing aloud. What tone of voice would you use?

Identifying tone

To identify the tone of a piece of writing, you need to look at **word choice**, **content** and **structure**, e.g:

- Colloquial and slang terms give writing a more **conversational** tone, e.g. *in your face* or *street cred*.

- Writing in the 2nd person (*you*) is **more personal** than using the 3rd person (*he/she/it*).

- Exaggeration and jokes and puns add a **humorous** tone.

- Lots of short, direct sentences in an argument text may give it a **hard-hitting** tone.

- Long sentences and paragraphs often add a more **serious** tone.

Formality

Formal language gives writing a **serious** tone. It:

- follows all the rules of English grammar

- uses more difficult or technical words, e.g. *institutions* or *population*

- uses more complex sentences, e.g. *Although he became king in October, it was not until December that …*

- is often impersonal, e.g. *Latest figures show …* or *Steps are being taken to …*

Informal language gives writing a **lighter** tone. It:

- includes slang or colloquialisms, e.g. *cool* or *ain't*

- includes more contractions, e.g. *isn't, can't* or *won't*

- is more personal, e.g. *You could think about …*

- uses simpler words, including 'fillers', e.g. *well* or *yes, but …*

Question

Re-read the passage on page 25.

(a) Give three examples of formal language.
(b) How does the formal tone suit the purpose of the piece?

Answer

level 7

(a) The phrase 'voluntary euthanasia' is high level and formalises the subject matter. You would only read this in formal writing.

Some of the sentences are quite complex, such as the one beginning 'Furthermore, there are some religious people ...'. Complex sentences like this are typical of formal language.

The connective at the beginning of this sentence ('furthermore') is very high level and formal and leads the reader through the argument.

(b) It is a discussion text on a serious issue – euthanasia – so formal language suits its purpose.

Comment

This answer gets full marks. The student has chosen two good examples and shown an understanding of the purpose of the writing.

Did You Know?

Standard English is the name given to the kind of English you are taught to write in schools. Hardly anyone speaks it, though, except newsreaders on the TV or radio.

Spot Check

1 Describe the two different tones in these pieces of advice:
   – *It is important for everyone's health that they drink eight glasses of water each day.*
   – *Can you up your water intake by drinking up to eight glasses a day?*

2 Arrange in order of formality:
   – *It's really nice.*
   – *It is perfectly delightful.*
   – *That's wicked, man.*

The questions

Some short questions ask you to **find information** in the extract.
Often this is the first question asked about an extract.

Here are some examples (about the extract opposite):

1 How long has Ginger been sleeping rough?

2 What part of the country is Link from?

Answering the questions

- You have to **scan** the extract to look for the information you want. Sometimes you are told where to look, e.g. *In the first paragraph, find …*

- Give **only** the information you are asked for, e.g. (question 1):

  - *Six or seven months* ✓

  - *Ginger has been sleeping rough for six or seven months.* ✓

  - *Ginger has been sleeping rough for six or seven months. He comes from Birmingham.* ✗

- Simply copy the key word or phrase that you are asked for. Don't add extra information. You don't need to write in complete sentences.

Top Tip!
- You can rephrase the text to show that you understand it, but it's easier simply to **copy the key word or phrase** that you are asked for.
- Don't spend too long on these questions – they are worth only 1 or 2 marks.

Did You Know?
Rudyard Kipling, the author of *Jungle Book*, once painted his golf balls red so that he could play in the snow.

Spot Check
Look at these statements about questions that ask you to find information. Are they true or false?
1 You don't have to write complete sentences.
2 You need to know information that isn't in the extract.
3 They are worth a lot of marks.
4 You have to put the information in the extract into your own words.

Read this passage about Link, a teenager who finds himself homeless in London. It describes his first night in a street doorway.

I'd just wriggled into my sleeping-bag and dropped my head on my pack when he arrived. I heard these footsteps and thought, keep going. Go past. Please go past, but he didn't. The footsteps stopped and I knew he was looking down at me. I opened my eyes. He was just a shadow framed in the doorway. "This your place?" I croaked. Stupid question. He was going to say yes even if it wasn't, right? What I should have said was piss off. I wondered how big he was.

 "No, you're right, mate." He sounded laid back, amiable. "Just shove up a bit so I can spread my roll." I obliged and he settled himself beside me, so close we were almost touching. It felt good to be with someone. Now, if anybody else turned up it wouldn't matter. There were two of us. I felt I ought to say something so I said, "Been doing this long?" hoping he wouldn't be offended.

 "Six, seven months," he said. "You?"

 "First night."

 He chuckled. "I can tell. Where you from?"

 "Up north."

 "Brum, me."

 "I can tell." It was a risk, this crack about his accent, but he only chuckled again. "Name's Ginger," he said, and waited.

(From *Stone Cold*, by Robert Swindells)

1 What was Link's reaction when he heard footsteps?

2 Link asks Ginger, "This your place?" Why does he think it was a 'stupid question'?

3 What reason does Link give for feeling good about sharing the doorway with someone else?

1 He wanted the person to keep going.

2 Because Ginger was going to say Yes even if it wasn't his place.

3 If anybody else turned up, it wouldn't matter.

The questions

Some questions ask you to **interpret** the text. This means 'reading between the lines'. You need to understand what the author is **suggesting** or **implying** – these things will not be stated clearly in the extract.

Here are some examples of questions like this (all relate to the passage on page 29):

1 Write down two words or phrases which show Link is unsure about the right things to say or do.

2 Give two reasons why Link may have wanted the footsteps to 'keep going'.

3 What impression do you get of Ginger? Refer to the text in your answer.

4 'It was a risk, this crack about his accent.' What does Link mean?

Answering the questions

- Sometimes you are simply asked to scan for the right **words or phrases**, e.g. (question 1):

  'Stupid question', 'I felt I ought to say something'

- Sometimes you need to give a **longer answer**, e.g. (question 2):

  Link may have wanted the footsteps to keep going because he was frightened of being moved on by the police. Or he may have thought he was going to be attacked.

- You may be asked to **refer to the text** in your answer. This means quoting the relevant bit and explaining what it shows, e.g. (question 3):

  Ginger seems to be very laid back. He doesn't pretend that it is his place. Instead he says, 'No, you're right, mate'. He chuckles when he's talking to Link.

Top Tip!

- If the passage is a **story**, try to **imagine** what the characters are thinking or feeling. Getting 'under their skin' will help you answer this sort of question.
- When reading a **non-fiction** passage, think about what a piece of information is really implying. What consequences does it have?

Spot Check

1 What does 'imply' mean?
2 What does 'reading between the lines' mean?
3 'You can give your own opinion when answering this sort of question?' True or false?

We get different impressions of Link's state of mind in this passage (see page 29).

Complete the following table by writing down three more quotations from the extract and explaining what each of them suggests about Link's state of mind.

Quotation	What this suggests about Link's state of mind
"This your place?" I croaked.	He is worried that he has taken someone else's sleeping place.

Answer

Quotation	What this suggests about Link's state of mind
"This your place?" I croaked.	He is worried that he has taken someone else's sleeping place.
I wondered how big he was.	Link was anxious in case he was going to be attacked.
I felt I ought to say something.	He is nervous about leaving a silence between them.
Stupid question.	Link feels annoyed with himself.

Comment

This answer gets full marks because it gives three suitable quotations and describes what all three quotations suggest about Link's state of mind. The answer shows that the student really understands what is going on in the story.

Did YOU Know?

Bruno Hauptmann kidnapped and murdered a baby, and was sent to the electric chair in 1936. What gave him away was his habit of adding extra 'e's to the end of words. He did this in his ransom note.

The questions

Some questions ask you to comment on the way a writer **organises** the text. This means thinking about how it is put together. You could be asked about how the whole text is put together, or how certain features (the beginning, the ending, headings, etc.) are effective.

Here are some examples of questions like this (all relate to the passage on page 29):

1 Why does the writer use short sentences in the first paragraph and longer ones in the second paragraph?

2 Give two ways in which the writer draws the reader in at the beginning of this passage.

3 How does the writer create an atmosphere of tension in the first paragraph?

4 Explain why the writer has followed two long paragraphs with several short ones.

Answering the questions

- Sometimes you just have to give a **reason** for something, e.g. (question 1):

  The short sentences show that Link is tense. The longer sentences in the next paragraph show he is more relaxed.

- Sometimes you need to **refer to the text**, e.g. (question 2):

  The writer says 'he arrived' in the first sentence. We are not told who 'he' is, but we want to know, so this draws us in.

- Note that when you give a quotation, you often need to explain why you have used it. *The writer says 'he arrived' in the first sentence* is not enough on its own, because it doesn't explain the **effect** of the words quoted.

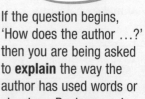

Top Tip!

If the question begins, 'How does the author …?' then you are being asked to **explain** the way the author has used words or structure. Back up each point with a quotation from the passage, and make sure you **explain** why the quotation has been used.

Spot Check

1 Why are paragraphs used in a text?
2 What kind of texts use subheadings, and why?
3 Why is the beginning of a text particularly important?

Read the final seven lines of the passage on page 29.

1 Why do the paragraphs suddenly become much shorter at this point? What effect does this have?

2 Explain why the writer has repeated the phrase 'I can tell' at the end of the passage.

> "Six, seven months," he said. "You?"
> "First night."
> He chuckled. "I can tell. Where you from?"
> "Up north."
> "Brum, me."
> "I can tell." It was a risk, this crack about his accent, but he only
> chuckled again. "Name's Ginger," he said, and waited.

Answer

1 The paragraphs become shorter because the characters are having a conversation. Each speech begins a new line. It suggests they are talking quickly, in short bursts, especially the very short sentences such as 'First night.'

2 Link repeats the same phrase that Ginger has used, as a joke. He is getting back at Ginger by using the same words.

Comment

This answer gets full marks because it explains clearly why the writer has organised the passage in these two ways. In describing the effect of the short paragraphs, the student has quoted from the extract to give an example.

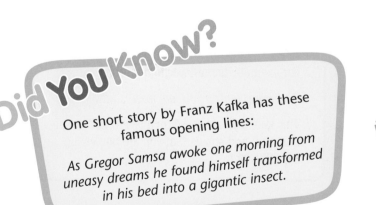

Did You Know?

One short story by Franz Kafka has these famous opening lines:

As Gregor Samsa awoke one morning from uneasy dreams he found himself transformed in his bed into a gigantic insect.

The questions

Some questions ask you to comment on the writer's **use of language** – the **meaning** of certain words, or the **effect** of certain words.
Here are some examples of questions like this (all relate to the passage opposite):

1 In the first sentence, what does 'mischievous little fellow' suggest that the writer feels about frost?

2 What is the effect of describing frost patterns as 'sparkling sculptures' (paragraph 2)?

3 How suitable is the image of a 'spiky white coat' to describe the effect of rime frost (paragraph 3)?

4 In the whole passage, how does the writer's choice of language make you feel that frost is something attractive?

Answering the questions

• Sometimes your answers will be quite short, e.g. (question 1):

It suggests that the writer thinks frost is fun and plays tricks on us.

• In the longer answers you need to **refer to the text**, e.g. (question 3):

The writer makes you feel frost is attractive by using the image of the artist or sculptor. In the first paragraph he 'paints intricate patterns', and in the third paragraph the patterns are described as 'delicate'. Both of the adjectives 'intricate' and 'delicate' make the patterns sound attractive. He is also described as making 'sparkling sculptures'.

Top Tip!

In your longer answers, it is often a good idea to refer to the words of the question in your answer. For example, the answer to question 3 begins

The writer makes you feel frost is attractive …

This keeps you focused on answering the question, and shows that you are answering the question!

Read this newspaper article. The author explores the legend of Jack Frost and explains how frost affects the landscape.

WEATHERWATCH

Every winter a mischievous little fellow persists in painting intricate patterns on cars, windows, leaves and rocks. Legend has it that Jack Frost was the son of the Norse god of wind, Kari. Originally he was known as Jokul [icicle] Frosti [frost], which became Jack Frost when he emigrated to the UK.

Cold, clear nights with a light wind blowing and temperatures close to freezing are perfect for Jack Frost. Valleys and hollows receive more visits because cold air sinks into low-lying areas. His favourite places to create his sparkling sculptures include rocky, glass or metal surfaces because they radiate heat and cool more quickly than the air surrounding them. Car windscreens are ideal.

Normally Jack Frost paints delicate, feather-like patterns, otherwise known as hoar frost.

He interlocks ice crystals, which grow outwards from a small seed, such as a tiny lump or scratch on the surface. But if the air is moist (often foggy) and the wind a little more breezy then Jack Frost switches to the rime frost technique. Grainy needles grow outwards, lining themselves up with the wind direction and giving structures like electricity pylons a spiky white coat.

Not everyone blames Jack Frost for their white windscreens. In Russia people say that Father Frost has been – a blacksmith who forges great chains of ice to bind water to earth each winter. Meanwhile in Germany Mother Frost is reputed to have been shaking out white feathers from her bed.

Kate Ravilious

(Copyright Guardian Newspapers Limited 2005)

1 Why does the author use the word 'emigrated' at the end of paragraph 1?

2 How suitable is the image of a 'spiky white coat' to describe the effect of rime frost (paragraph 3)?

Did YOU Know?

The longest word in the English language is 'smiles'. (There is a mile between the first and last letter!)

Answer

1 The author uses the word 'emigrated' because she wants to suggest that Jack Frost was born in another country, and changed his name when he came to the UK.

2 The image of the 'spiky white coat' is very suitable because it shows how everything is covered in white, as if it is wearing a coat. Also the fur on a coat is a bit like the needles of frost.

level
7

Explaining purpose and effect

The questions

Some questions ask you to comment on the **purpose** or **point of view** of the writer. They may also ask you to explain the **effect** of the text.

Here are some examples of questions like this (all relate to the passage on page 35):

1 Suggest a reason why the author begins her explanation of frost by describing the legend of Jack Frost.

2 Does the author like frost? Explain your answer.

3 The writer talks about Jack Frost throughout the article, not frost. What effect does this have?

4 How does the writer try to make the reader like frost in this passage?

Answering the questions

- Sometimes your answers will be quite short, e.g. (question 1):

  The author wants to grab the reader's interest at the start with a story.

- In the longer answers you need to **refer to the text**, e.g. (question 2):

  The author seems to like frost a lot. She treats it almost as a person, calling it Jack Frost and saying that 'he' has 'favourite places to create' in. She also describes the effect of frost in a positive way, with adjectives such as 'sparkling' and 'delicate'.

Question

In the passage on page 35 the writer sets out to entertain the reader as well as to explain what frost is.

How does she entertain the reader? You should comment on:
- the topics covered
- the language used
- the way frost is referred to as Jack Frost.

Answer

Although this article basically aims to give the reader information and a bit of explanation about frost, it isn't written in a dull or lifeless way. To begin with, the author gives us a bit of interesting information about the legend of Jack Frost, which she returns to at the end. She also describes two different types of frost, which is fascinating.

The language is very well chosen to entertain the reader. There are lots of powerful adjectives (e.g. 'intricate', 'sparkling'). The author deliberately describes things in an interesting way, for example she says 'Valleys and hollows receive more visits' instead of 'You get a lot of frost in valleys and hollows'. This brings the passage to life.

The main way in which the author entertains the reader is by referring to frost as Jack Frost. Frost is not just a person, but an artist who deliberately creates pictures and sculptures. He is described as choosing different methods depending on the weather: 'if the air is moist ... then Jack Frost switches to the rime frost technique'. We imagine a person doing all this, not just something in nature.

Comment

This answer is above a level 7. It shows a clear understanding of the purpose of the text, and explains how the writer uses different techniques to achieve her purpose. It covers all the three areas suggested in the bullet points. It gives evidence from the text to back up the views, quoting where relevant and showing the precise effect of the quotations. It is very well organised and expressed throughout.

Top Tip!

The longer questions, which carry more marks, may give a **bullet point list** of topics to include in your answer. To get top marks you need to cover all the suggestions. They can also give you a structure for your answer – devote a short paragraph to each one.

Above level 7

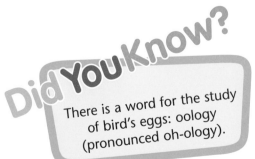
Did You Know?
There is a word for the study of bird's eggs: oology (pronounced oh-ology).

If you want to move from level 6 to level 7 you need to show these skills.
(All examples relate to the passage on page 35.)

Answer all parts of the question

- Read the question **carefully** and answer it **exactly**.

- If it asks you to comment on a feature through the **whole text**, then make sure you give a spread of evidence across the text.

- If several **bullet point** 'prompts' are given, cover each point in your answer.

Show in detail how the writer achieves an effect

- Don't just describe an effect by quoting the relevant part of the passage. Add a **comment** showing how the effect is achieved. For example, if you are asked to comment on the image 'forges great chains of ice', you could say, *It is a metaphor which suggests the icy grip on the landscape is long-lasting, strong and hard.*

Show how the features of the text suit its purpose

- Be aware not only of language or structural features, but also of how they are chosen deliberately to suit the **aim** of the writing. For example, you could comment, *The author personifies frost in order to make her explanation/information text more entertaining.*

Identify how texts are organised for a particular purpose or viewpoint

- You need to think about the **structure** of the text in terms of how it helps the writer achieve their purpose. Do the paragraphs get shorter to increase the tension? Does each section begin with a rhetorical question to engage the reader's interest? For example, you could say, *The author has used the device of personifying frost consistently through the article to make it coherent (bind it together) and attractive to read.*

Top Tip!

Look carefully at the key word in the question. Questions beginning 'What' are often asking for information. Questions beginning 'How' are often asking you to describe how language is used.

Read the passage on page 35 again.

(a) How has the writer structured the article overall?
(b) How does the structure help the author's purpose?

Answer

(a) The author has used a different paragraph for each topic. The first one talks about the legend of Jack Frost. The second paragraph describes different places and weather conditions suitable for frost, whereas the third paragraph describes two different types of frost. The final paragraph returns to the legend of Jack Frost, but looks at how the story is told in different countries.

(b) The author organises her article very clearly in this way because she is giving information and explaining how something works. Clear organisation is important in this kind of writing. She sandwiches the more scientific material in between information about legends, which is very clever and satisfying: the author wants to entertain us, not just give dry information.

Above level 7

Comment

This answer is above a level 7. The student shows a high level of awareness of both how the text is structured and how this structure contributes to the overall effect of the piece and the aim of the writer. Every aspect of the question is covered, and detail is given. There is no need to quote from the article. The answer is well organised and well expressed.

Did YOU Know?

The dot on the letter 'i' is called a tipple.

Writing skills

Throughout your Key Stage 3 course, you will be assessed on your writing skills. This section of the book focuses on the different skills you will need to improve your writing and move up a level.

Different types of writing tasks

- Your teacher may give you two different styles of writing tasks to practise. A longer writing task and a shorter writing task.

- Both tasks give you some **background**, and suggest the sort of things you should include in your answer.

- Each writing task will have a different **purpose** and **form**. For example, you may be telling a story, writing a persuasive letter or composing a report.

Pages 52–3 (different forms) and 62–71 (different purposes).

Top Tip!

Try hard to spell words correctly. It could push you from a level 6 to a level 7.

What you get marks for

- **Composition and effect**
  This means the style, form and language that you use – how interesting the writing is, how well it fits the audience, how well the style and tone suits the purpose of the task, how varied and effective the vocabulary is.

  Pages 42–3, 46–9 and 52–3.

- **Sentence structure and punctuation**
  This means how well organised and varied your sentences are, and whether you have used punctuation to make your meaning clear.

  Pages 48–9 and 54–7.

- **Text structure and organisation**
  This means how well organised your whole text is, e.g. use of paragraphs and the order of your points.

  Pages 50–1.

- **Spelling**
  This is marked only in the shorter writing task.

  Pages 58–61.

Did You Know?

A **blend** is a word made up of the shortened form of two other words, e.g. **heli**port (**heli**copter + air**port**).

Timing and planning

- You should spend the first 15 minutes **planning** your longer writing task.

- You should spend the last 5 minutes **checking** what you have written – improving the spelling, punctuation and vocabulary. This will always gain you marks.

Pages 44–5.

Example

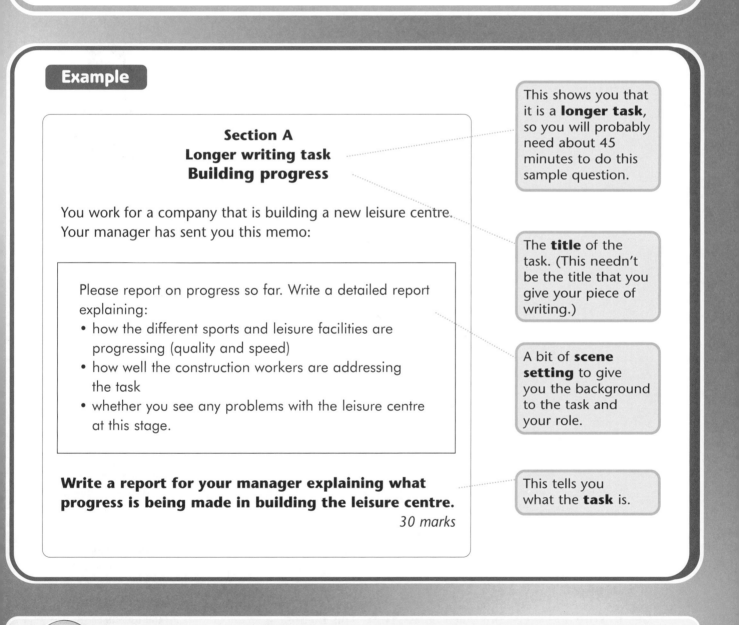

Section A
Longer writing task
Building progress

You work for a company that is building a new leisure centre. Your manager has sent you this memo:

Please report on progress so far. Write a detailed report explaining:
- how the different sports and leisure facilities are progressing (quality and speed)
- how well the construction workers are addressing the task
- whether you see any problems with the leisure centre at this stage.

Write a report for your manager explaining what progress is being made in building the leisure centre.

30 marks

This shows you that it is a **longer task**, so you will probably need about 45 minutes to do this sample question.

The **title** of the task. (This needn't be the title that you give your piece of writing.)

A bit of **scene setting** to give you the background to the task and your role.

This tells you what the **task** is.

Spot Check

True or false?
1 Composition means how neat your work is.
2 You get extra marks for correct spelling.
3 Text structure and organisation is about your handwriting.
4 You should spend 15 minutes planning your longer writing task.

Before you plan and write, you need to think carefully about what to write and how to write it. That means asking yourself these questions:

What am I writing?

- Look at the **format** word in the question paper, e.g. Write a **letter**, an **account**, the first chapter of your **story**, a **leaflet**, a **speech**, a **report**, a **newspaper article**.

- Keep this format in mind as you plan and write. Most formats have their own conventions.

- Now identify the **content**, or **topic**, that you have to write about, e.g. (a letter) describing your **visit**, or (a report) describing your project.

Pages 52–3.

Why am I writing?

- Work out your **purpose** in writing.

- **Stories** are easy – they should entertain.

- For non-fiction, though, you must look for the key word in the question: **inform**, **explain**, **describe**, **persuade**, **argue**, **advise**, **analyse**, **review**, **comment**.

Pages 66–71.

Who am I writing for?

- Keep your **audience** in mind when you plan and write. You have to adjust what you are writing to what they want to read.

- The audience is not the examiners, but the **person** (or people) indicated **in the question**, e.g. your fellow classmates, the head teacher, the prime minister, your cousin in America, the manager of a factory.

What is my role?

- You will often be told to imagine you are a **particular person**, e.g. a local resident, a head teacher, a newspaper reporter. This is your **role**.

- Each role will demand its own **voice**. This could be anything from 'very personal and friendly' to 'very distant and informal'.

- The voice you choose also depends on the **purpose** and **audience** of your piece.

- **Get in role** and keep your voice **consistent**. This means:
  - not changing your **point of view**, e.g. from student to teacher, or from 3rd person to 1st person
  - not changing the **formality** of the language unless for deliberate effect
  - not changing the **tone**, e.g. from light-hearted to serious.

Top Tip!

Look at the context when you are told to 'comment'. For example:
- 'Write a letter commenting on the proposals to close the park' means **arguing** for or against the proposals.
- 'Write a report commenting on the results of your survey' means **analysing** the results.

Pages 26–7.

Look again at the writing task from page 41.

How does thinking about purpose, audience and role help you approach the task?

> ### Section A
> ### Longer writing task
> ### Building progress
>
> You work for a company that is building a new leisure centre. Your manager has sent you this memo:
>
> > Please report on progress so far. Write a detailed report explaining:
> > • how the different sports and leisure facilities are progressing (quality and speed)
> > • how well the construction workers are addressing the task
> > • whether you see any problems with the leisure centre at this stage.
>
> **Write a report for your manager explaining what progress is being made in building the leisure centre.**
>
> *30 marks*

The title of the task gives a flavour of the **voice** you should take on. Here the title is formal, informative and serious.

This is your **role** – you work for a building company. You need to keep this role going through the writing.

This list suggests the **content** of your report. You could **organise** the report into three sections like this.

In the task, you are given:
• the **form** of the writing (a report)
• the **purpose** of the writing (to explain)
• the **audience** of the writing (your manager).
So the report should be clear, formal, logical and polite.

Did You Know?

The most common word used in conversation is 'I'.

Spot Check

1 Match the question with the correct purpose.

Question	Purpose
a Give your views on …	To inform or describe
b Tell x how to …	To persuade
c Give an account of …	To instruct
d Inspire your team …	To argue

2 What does 'keeping your voice consistent' mean?

Planning is important

- You must spend time planning the answers to both writing tasks.

- Planning makes you **think carefully** about the task, instead of writing the first thing that comes into your head.

- It improves the **content** of your writing. You have time to think up good ideas.

- It also improves the **structure** of your writing. You can organise it instead of just rambling on.

Top Tip!

Read carefully the **detail** given in the background to the question. It will give you lots of ideas for:
(a) what to write about
(b) how to structure your answer.

Planning for the longer task

- If you are doing a longer task, then it's good practice to spend **at least 15 minutes** planning your answer.

- Your teacher may give you a planning grid, which will often supply the basic structure for your writing. You may need to adjust this to make a complete plan (see page 45).

Planning for the shorter task

- You are not given a planning page for the shorter writing task. However, make sure you spend at least 5 minutes **thinking and planning** before you start writing.

Pages 64–71 (planning tools).

- You can use the question paper or some spare paper to draw up a **quick plan**.

- **Brainstorm** some key words and ideas first. Then develop these ideas and order them, using your own planning tool.

Spot Check

True or false?

1 You should start writing as soon as you can.
2 You should spend at least 5 minutes planning for the shorter writing task.
3 Planning helps you organise your writing more effectively.
4 Planning doesn't improve the content of your writing.

Examples

A A planning page for the longer writing task 'Building program' (see page 41).

How sports and leisure facilities are progressing

- swimming pool finished
- grounds being landscaped
- tennis courts hardly started
- main hall under construction

How workers are addressing the task

- most very hard-working
- those on outdoor facilities often absent
- complaints about harsh managers
- staff holidays will mean further delays

Any problems with the leisure centre at this stage

- some staffing problems need sorting out: extra cover for holidays, investigate complaints
- delays to outdoor courts
- wrong tiles used in main hall

> You can follow this basic structure for your writing, but you will need to add an introduction.

> The notes are short and simple. The order of points in the boxes can be changed when you write your final version.

> This could act as your conclusion.

B A planning page for the question: 'Write the beginning of a short story about someone who has been left on their own.'

Notes for description of character

- astronaut – unnamed (1st person)
- normally cool and calm
- dressed in full gear, heavy helmet, etc.

Notes for description of setting

- space station
- set in future, 2500
- huge area, lots of levels
- vast banks of computers
- completely empty – very eerie
- station circling a new, black planet

Notes on what happens in the story

- I wake up, after a year's 'frozen' sleep
- all companions gone – feelings of being alone
- explore space station, signs that it was left in a hurry
- computer tells me we're being sucked into dark planet

> This planning page helps you gather ideas for a **story**.

> Jot ideas in the boxes as they occur to you.

> Only this panel can be used to **structure** the story.

The power of words

A wide vocabulary helps your writing in so many ways:

* It means you **avoid repeating** words.

* It makes your writing **more interesting**.

* You can be **more precise** about the meaning or the effect.

* You can use the **appropriate** word for the purpose or audience.

More interesting

* Adjectives and adverbs improve your descriptions, e.g.
  He lay the axe on the ground. ✗
  He lay his battered axe wearily on the ground. ✓

* Longer, more difficult words are often impressive, e.g.
  an atrocious attack, un unacceptable request.

More precise

* Try to avoid nouns and verbs that are very general, e.g.
  She ran to the shops. ✗
  She jogged all the way to the newsagent's on the corner. ✓

* The exact noun or verb you use creates a particular effect:
  The cat lounged in the summer house.
  The cat whimpered in the shed.

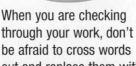

Top Tip!

When you are checking through your work, don't be afraid to cross words out and replace them with better ones. You will get marks for using a higher level word, even if it is spelt incorrectly.

More appropriate

Choose words to suit the **purpose** and **audience** of your writing:

* more **formal** words for a discussion piece, e.g. *locate, conclusion*

* some **informal** words for a teenage audience, e.g. *cool, kids*

* **emotive** words in persuasive writing, e.g. *broken-hearted, abandoned*

* **technical** words in information writing, e.g. *species, habitat*

Spot Check

1 Think of four alternatives for the word 'bad'.
2 Rank them in order of 'badness' (the worst at the end).
3 Which of these words would you **not** use in a formal discussion?
wonderful, spectacular, fab, delightful, stimulating

Stylistic devices

- To achieve higher levels, examiners will be looking for some stylistic devices:
  - **alliteration**, e.g. *the ridiculous rodent*
  - **imagery** – **similes** (*as dull as a grey Sunday*) or **metaphors** (*his frustration boiled over into fury*)
  - **extended metaphor** – when an image is developed for a few sentences, e.g. *She attacked her dinner mercilessly. She speared each potato in turn. Then the sausages were put to the sword …*

Example

This is a level 7 student's review.

Read the examiner's comments on the vocabulary used.

level
7

Philip Pullman's spellbinding 'His Dark Materials' trilogy ends with 'The Amber Spyglass', which keeps up the superb quality of writing shown in 'Northern Lights' and 'The Subtle Knife', the first two titles in the sequence. Will and Lyra, the two children at the heart of the books, have become separated, and are being hunted down by terrible powers. Can they find each other and their friends? Can they complete their mysterious quest before it is too late? The great rebellion against the dark powers that enslave Lyra's world is nearing its climax.

The plot, then, has all the power and surprise of a great adventure story. The pace of the story never lets up. What is most striking, however, is the depth of the characterisation. Lord Asriel, Mrs Coulter, Iorek Byrnison (the king of the armoured bears) and, above all, Will and Lyra themselves are beautifully drawn characters who fully convince, even though the story is effectively science-fiction. The relationship between Will and Lyra moved me to tears.

Comment

- **Correct terms** used confidently (*trilogy, plot, characterisation*)
- More **interesting** and **precise** than *in the books*
- Good use of qualifiers (**adverbs**) to add precision and force (*beautifully, fully, effectively*)
- **Powerful** and effective **adjectives** (*spellbinding, terrible, mysterious*)

Did YOU Know?

Making your sentences interesting

Vary the type of your sentences

- Most sentences are **statements**, e.g. *The CD cost £14.99.*

- You can add **variety** by including other types of sentence:
  - **questions**, e.g. *How much does this CD cost?*
  - **exclamations**, e.g. *Only £14.99!*
  - **commands**, e.g. *Buy this CD for me!*

Vary the length of your sentences

- **Short sentences** often have only one clause, e.g.
  Tammy borrowed £5 from her brother.
  They are useful in instructions and straightforward information text. They can also add impact after a series of longer sentences.

- **Compound sentences** combine clauses with 'and' or 'but', e.g.
  Tammy borrowed £5 from her brother and didn't pay him back.
  They can make your sentences longer, but avoid structures like … *and … and … and then …*

- **Complex sentences** show the links between the clauses clearly by using **connectives** such as 'although' and 'when', e.g. *Tammy borrowed £5 from her brother since she had left her purse behind.*

- Include **relative clauses** (to add information), e.g.
  Tammy borrowed £5 from her brother, who never let her forget it.

Other kinds of variety

- **Begin** your sentences in different ways:
  He went to the arcade. He played on the games. He … ✗
  He went to the arcade. After he'd played on the games, he … ✓

- Expand your nouns with **noun phrases**:
  She was given an alarm clock. ✗
  She was given an alarm clock designed to leap about instead of making a sound. ✓

- Include **adverbial phrases**, e.g. *in the meantime, for better or for worse.*

- Make your verbs **impersonal** (e.g. *It is likely …*), conditional, (e.g. *If you heat the water …*) or passive (e.g. *The water was heated*).

- You can **embed clauses**, e.g.
  Koala bears, although they look cuddly, are fierce creatures.

Top Tip!

Remember that every sentence must make sense on its own. This almost always means that every sentence has a verb. Only break this rule occasionally for deliberate effect. *Like this!*

Did You Know?

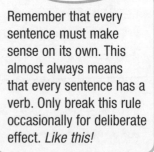

You should never write 'would of' or 'should of'. The correct form is 'would have' or 'should have', e.g. *I would have got full marks marks if I hadn't written 'would of'.*

Example

Look again at the level 7 student's review from page 47.
Read the examiner's comments on the **sentence structure** used.

Philip Pullman's spellbinding 'His Dark Materials' trilogy ends with 'The Amber Spyglass', which keeps up the superb quality of writing shown in 'Northern Lights' and 'The Subtle Knife', the first two titles in the sequence. Will and Lyra, the two children at the heart of the books, have become separated, and are being hunted down by terrible powers. Can they find each other and their friends? Can they complete their mysterious quest before it is too late? The great rebellion against the dark powers that enslave Lyra's world is nearing its climax.

The plot, then, has all the power and surprise of a great adventure story. The pace of the story never lets up. What is most striking, however, is the depth of the characterisation. Lord Asriel, Mrs Coulter, Iorek Byrnison (the king of the armoured bears) and, above all, Will and Lyra themselves are beautifully drawn characters who fully convince, even though the story is effectively science-fiction. The relationship between Will and Lyra moved me to tears.

Comment

- Effective use of **relative clause** to add information.
- **Connectives** embedded in sentence vary the rhythm, e.g. *then, however*.
- **Embedded phrase** for variety.
- **Questions** add interest and variety.
- Good use of **shorter sentences** to break up the flow and add impact .

Spot Check

1 Combine these sentences to make them more interesting:
   Kevin took the bus to town. He pushed through the crowds. He didn't want to miss the start of the film.
2 Now do it again in a different way!
3 Rewrite this sentence using the passive:
   Midge's mother gave him a hard time.

Paragraphs

- A paragraph is a group of sentences on one topic. Paragraphs are used to **organise** your writing and to help the reader **follow your ideas**.

- You begin a new paragraph when you talk about a **new point**, **character**, **place** or **time**.

- Paragraphs are also used to show **different speakers** in a passage of dialogue.

- You show it's a new paragraph by leaving a line space, or starting the new line slightly in from the margin.

Ordering paragraphs

- This is where **planning** is vital. Each main item in your plan will often become a separate paragraph.

- Number the items on your plan to give you a **sensible order** for your paragraphs.

- The order will depend on the **purpose** of your writing, e.g. **chronological** order (for a recount), **logical** order (for an explanation) or order of **importance** (for an argument).

Pages 44–5.

Beginnings and endings

- The **first paragraph** must be effective. It may be a general introduction, or it may grab the reader by creating a mystery or a shock, or by addressing the reader directly.

- Make your **final paragraph** a definite ending. It will leave a good impression. Techniques include:
  – referring back to the beginning (tying the piece together)
  – a clever twist
  – a sharp one-sentence paragraph
  – a question.

Top Tip!

When checking your work, you can add an insertion mark and write (NP) where you want to start a new paragraph. Or you can do the opposite – draw a box round text and link it to the previous paragraph.

Signalling where you are going

- Use **topic sentences** to start each paragraph. These give the main point of the paragraph. Then develop the point by adding reasons, examples, etc.

- Use **connectives** and **signposts** to show where your sentences are going, e.g. *Yet ...* (here's an opposite point), *The following day ...* (to tell you when), *Other people disagree ...* (to tell you who).

This example of an advice text gains a level 7 for its organisation and structure.

How to deal with rejection

When a relationship breaks up, it can be a very painful experience, especially if it happens suddenly. You can feel a shock, almost as if your friend has died.

Logical point to put at the beginning.

If the relationship was a really good one, it's normal to feel grief that it's over. So don't think that it's wrong to get some of the grief out of your system by having a good cry.

Each paragraph covers a separate point.

If the relationship is clearly over, don't waste time trying to patch it up. If you go round pleading with your ex-boyfriend/girlfriend to take you back, you're only prolonging the agony. Doing so is more likely to turn them off than win them back.

Most paragraphs give the main point first (topic sentence). Then they develop the point, e.g. with a reason or example.

Also, one thing people do when they're rejected is to ask themselves what went wrong. Remember that relationships end for all sorts of reasons, and it's hardly ever one person's fault.

Connectives and signposts show how the ideas are structured.

Finally, don't worry that you'll never make another relationship. When a relationship ends, it can be difficult to imagine there'll be others. But there will be!

Effective final paragraph.

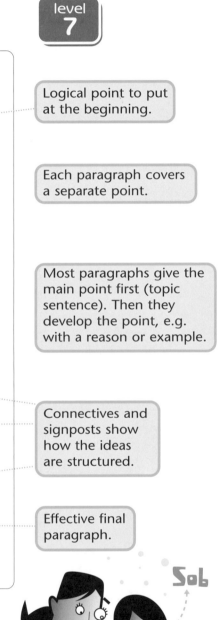

Sob

Did You Know?

The Unfortunates (1969) is a novel supplied in a box. Its author, Bryan Johnson, provides the first and last chapters but presents the rest as single pages that can be read in any order.

Spot Check

1 Give three reasons why you would start a new paragraph.
2 'You need a new paragraph every 10 or 15 lines.' True or false?
3 What makes an effective beginning? Name two techniques.
4 Explain what a topic sentence is.

Letters

- **Lay out** the letter properly.

Page 53.

- Most letters need a **formal** style, e.g. a letter of complaint, a letter to a newspaper, or to apply for a job.

- Some letters will be more **informal**, e.g. to a friend or relative.

Pages 26–7 (formality).

Newspaper stories

- Write in a **clear but lively** style: you need to entertain as well as inform your readers.

- Use **short paragraphs** and **short sentences**.

- The first paragraph often gives the main information – answering the questions 'who', 'what', 'where' and 'when'. Later paragraphs give further details.

- Include **quotes** from people involved, or comments from experts.

- Add a snappy **headline**.

Leaflets

Leaflets usually have to get their point(s) over quickly, clearly and persuasively. Think about:

- **presentation** – bullet points and subheadings are common devices to break up the text. Leave spaces for graphics, pictures or logos.

- **text structure** – short paragraphs and sentences; headings to guide the reader through the text.

- **style** – it should be clear and simple for information or advice. Use emotive words, personal pronouns, etc. for a persuasive leaflet.

> **Top Tip!**
>
> When writing a leaflet, don't waste time on design. For example, draw an empty box and add a label (*picture of …*) rather than spending time drawing an actual picture.

Pages 70–1 (persuasive techniques).

Reports

- Most reports are **factual** and **formal**, like a school report or evaluation. They use **clear** and **formal** language, and a **reasonable** tone.

- **Impersonal phrases** are common, e.g. *It is preferable …* or *A good example is …*

- Verbs are often in the **passive**, e.g. *Steps are being taken …* or *The product was assessed …*

- **Modal verbs** are used for evaluation, e.g. *It should take …* or *The manager must learn …*

- The **structure** will be **logical** – introduction, then main points in order of importance, and summary at the end.

Did You Know?

One of the shortest letters was written by the novelist Victor Hugo. Wanting to know how people were reacting to his latest novel, he wrote to his publishers: '?' They replied: '!'

Speeches

- Remember that the audience will be **listening** to the speech, so try and imagine someone reading it aloud. Some good **sound effects** include:
  - **repetition**, e.g. *It's time to protest, and to protest with force.*
  - **alliteration**, e.g. *The proposal is dangerous and destructive.*
  - **lists of three**, e.g. *... for a better, fairer and more prosperous future.*
  - **varying the length** of your sentences for effect.

Pages 48–9.

- Speeches are full of **rhetorical techniques**.

Pages 70–1.

Example

Note how this letter is set out.

> 64 Queensbury Road
> Newtown
> Yorks YO3 4BX *— your address here*
>
> 15 September 2006 *— date*
>
> Gem Jewellers Ltd
> 48 High Street *— address of person you are writing to*
> Newtown
> Yorks YO1 5FD
>
> Dear Sir or Madam *— formal beginning, used if you don't know the name*
>
> I wish to complain about the service that I received last Saturday. *— clear statement of purpose at the start of the letter*
>
> (MAIN TEXT HERE)
>
> I look forward to hearing from you. *— You can also use 'Yours sincerely' here.*
>
> Yours faithfully
>
> *Kara Butler*
> KARA BUTLER *— full name, both signed and printed (in capitals)*

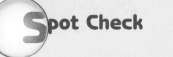

pot Check

Which of these phrases would you include in a letter, and which would you include in a speech?
1 With reference to your advert ...
2 Are we so bad? Are we so mad?
3 Dear Sir
4 I stand before you this evening ...
5 I look forward to hearing from you
6 Listen to reason.

Basic rules

- Every sentence must make complete sense on its own, so it must contain a verb:
  - *Twenty minutes on the trampoline.* ✗
  - *She was on the trampoline for 20 minutes.* ✓

- Every sentence must begin with a **capital letter**.

- Capitals are also used for **proper names**, e.g. *Raj, Ipswich, Nike, Robston College.*

- Every sentence must **end** with a **full stop**, a **question mark** or an **exclamation mark**.

Punctuation for adding text

- A **dash** adds a short bit of information, e.g.
  I put it here – no, here.
  Do not overuse dashes in this way.

- A **colon** introduces a list, e.g.
  These are our demands: £10,000 in cash, a getaway car …

- A **colon** also **introduces a clause** that leads on from or explains another clause, e.g.
  She was scared: it was dark and very late.

- A **semi-colon** links two clauses that are equally important, e.g.
  Ben liked running; Laura preferred swimming.

- You can **mark off extra information** by using dashes, brackets or commas:
  The culprit – or so it appeared – had slipped away.
  The culprit (or so it appeared) had slipped away.

Pages 56–7.

Apostrophes

- An apostrophe is used where words have been **shortened**, e.g.
  haven't (have not), *I'm* (I am), *he's* (he is), *let's* (let us), *they're* (they are). Note that the apostrophe is put where the missing letter should be.

- Apostrophes also tell you who **owns something**:
  - for **singular**, add apostrophe + **s**, e.g. *Brett's car, United's win*
  - for **plural**, add the apostrophe after the **s**, e.g. *a friends' gathering*

- Do not confuse apostrophes with speech marks.

Top Tip!

Remember that 'its' is used to show ownership (like 'his' and 'hers'), e.g. *She pulled its tail.* 'It's' stands for 'it is', e.g. *It's raining.*

This level 6 writing has some correct punctuation, but needs to improve its range to get a level 7.

level
6

Have you heard people say that soaps are just like real life? However, they are not nearly as realistic as real life, for several reasons. First of all, people die (or disappear) far more often in soaps. This is because of the actors' desire to leave the series after a period. If a key figure wants to leave, the producer has only two options. One is to kill him off, the other is divorce. Secondly, there is always something happening in characters' lives in soaps, whereas in real life it's actually quite boring. The scriptwriters have to make the show exciting to hold the viewers' attention.

> Could add a semi-colon here instead of beginning a new sentence.

> Could rephrase with a colon:
> '… two options: to kill him off or get him divorced.'

Did You Know?

The wrong use of an apostrophe in words that are just plurals is known as the 'greengrocer's apostrophe'. This is because it is so common to see signs like this at greengrocers' stalls.

Apple's half price

Spot Check

1 When do you need to use a capital letter?
2 Add the punctuation to this sentence:
   graemes mobile rang it was paula calling from oxford
3 Correct the punctuation in this sentence:
   'Its endless is'nt it!' she said – looking at: the minute's go by.
4 What is the difference between a colon and a semi-colon?

What is a comma?

The comma is a very useful and common punctuation mark. It is used in many different ways to **separate words**, **phrases and clauses** in a sentence. Using the comma well in your writing shows:
– that you can **organise** your sentences, so that their meaning is clear.
– that you can use punctuation accurately.

Separating words and phrases

- The comma must be used to **separate items in a list**:
  Please put all clothes, books, swimming and sporting equipment, mobile phones and other personal belongings in the lockers provided.
  – Note that the final item before 'and' (*mobile phones*) does not need a comma after it.
  – Note also that the comma comes after phrases (*swimming and sporting equipment*), not just words.

- The comma is used to **separate a phrase** that gives extra information about something:
  The third from the right, the woman in the hat, is the winner!

- The comma is often used **after words** or phrases that **begin sentences** e.g.
  Finally, However, Two days later, After all,

Separating clauses

- The comma is used to **separate clauses** (the main parts of a sentence):
  Although Keith ran as fast as he could, he still came last.
  Rebecca agreed to look after the dog, which was the worst decision she had ever made.

Things to avoid

- Do not put a comma between the subject and verb of a clause, even if the subject is very long:
  The third, final and most important point of all, is that we did our best. ✗
  The third, final and most important point of all is that we did our best ✓

- Think about what really links the clauses of a sentence. Often using a comma is not the best form of punctuation:
  To display web pages you need software called a browser, this converts the coded pages into a form that you can read on the computer. ✗
  Here the second clause is just 'tagged on'. You should use a **colon** or a **relative clause** instead of a comma, or start a new sentence:
  To display web pages you need software called a browser. This converts the coded pages into a form that you can read on the computer. ✓

Top Tip!
Do not overuse commas. Think about using other punctuation marks as well.

Example

Look at how one student has used commas in this piece of writing.

> Lots of girls want to look like the celebrities they see on TV. But celebrities have to look amazing: it's what they are paid to do. Unlike ordinary people, they have the time and money to achieve that perfect look. Most girls would look just as fantastic if they had personal trainers, beauticians, stylists and dieticians at their fingertips. Remember, too, that celebrities use top photographers, who are trained to get the best out of their subject. So don't judge your looks against photographs of top models, as it simply isn't a fair comparison.

A colon here is better than a comma.

Full stops (and new sentences) used correctly here instead of tagging on clauses with commas.

Comma separates items in a list.

Comma used to separate clauses.

Comment

This is a level 7 piece of writing. Commas are used accurately and effectively. They show the structure of the sentences clearly. Other punctuation is used instead of commas where necessary.

Did You Know?

The final chapter of James Joyce's novel *Ulysses* consists of eight enormous sentences. It goes on for over 60 pages and has no punctuation.

Spot Check

Add commas to these sentences:
1 He used the colours red white and blue to which he added yellow as an afterthought.
2 Lucy the youngest of the children is really the most important character.
3 Stuart was replaced at half-time which was the final straw.

Spelling: endings and beginnings

Plurals

Add **-s** to make the plural of a word, e.g. *house → houses, pool → pools*.

Exceptions:

- Words ending in **-ss**, **-sh**, **-ch**, **-x**: you add **-es**, e.g. *glasses, matches, foxes*.

- Words ending in consonant + **y**: you change **-y** to **-ies**, e.g. *lady → ladies, try → tries*.

- Words ending in **-f**: you usually change **-f** to **-ves**, e.g. *loaf → loaves, leaf → leaves*.

- Some words ending in **-o**: you add **-es**, e.g. *tomatoes, potatoes*.

- Some words don't follow these rules, e.g. *children, women, mice, sheep*.

Verbs

Add **-ing** or **-ed** to make different parts of the verb, e.g. *form → forming, formed; watch → watching, watched*.

Exceptions:

- Short verbs ending in vowel + consonant: you double the consonant, e.g. *drop → dropping; dropped, fit → fitting, fitted*.

- Longer verbs ending in vowel + consonant: double the consonant only if the emphasis is on the final syllable, e.g. *admit → admitting, prefer → preferring* but *benefit → benefiting*.

- Verbs ending in **-e**: you drop the **-e**, e.g. *decide → deciding, decided; state → stating, stated*.

- Many common verbs have different forms in the past tense, e.g. *fight → fought, begin → began, meet → met*.

Prefixes

- **Prefixes** are letters added at the **start** of a word to change its meaning. They do not change the spelling of the original word:

  - **in-**, **un-**, **im-**, **ir-**, **mis-** and **dis-** often form opposites, e.g. *invisible, unfair, impossible, mistrust*.
  - **pre-** and **fore-** mean 'in front' or 'before', e.g. *prefer, foreground*.

- Other prefixes include **ex-** and **re-** (again), e.g. *export, return*.

- **Suffixes** are letters added at the **end** of a word to change its meaning:
  - **-able**, **-ible** and **-uble** mean that something is possible, e.g. *legible, soluble.*
  - **-ful** means 'full of', e.g. *careful, peaceful.* (Note: not **-full**.)
  - **-less** means 'without', e.g. *careless, endless.*
  - **-ation**, **-ition**, **-ution** form a noun from a verb, e.g. *create → creation, pollute → pollution.*

- You drop a final **-e** before a suffix that begins with a vowel, e.g. *forgive + -able = forgivable*

Example

Look at these two versions of the same piece of writing. The student checked her spelling at the end of the test and made some corrections.

> I don't believe in horroscopes at all. No one knows about the future but Allah. Sometimes the prophesise come true but I think that it's considence. On Wendnesday the horoscope said: "Something aweful will happen today". I worried all day, and then I cought a cold. But surely everyday there's something bad that happens! They're just not believeable.

> I don't believe in horoscopes at all. No one knows about the future but Allah. Sometimes the prophecies come true but I think that it's coincidence. On Wednesday the horoscope said: "Something awful will happen today". I worried all day, and then I caught a cold. But surely every day there's something bad that happens! They're just not believable.

Did You Know?

'Dreamt' is the only English word ending in 'mt'.

Spot Check

1 Which are the incorrect plurals?
  churches, potatoes, flys, wolves, gasses
2 Add **-ing** and **-ed** to these verbs: *skate, skid, respect, benefit*
3 Give the past tense of these verbs: *dive, steal, travel, buy*
4 Use prefixes and suffixes to form two words from 'believe'.

Spelling strategies

Use a dictionary

- The best way to master spelling is to look words up in a **dictionary** while you are writing.

- Do *not* use spell checker programs. They don't tell you if a word is spelt correctly, only if it exists. And they make you a lazy speller.

- Note: you are not allowed to use a dictionary in the tests.

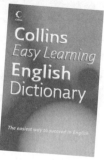

Collins
Easy Learning
English
Dictionary

The easiest way to succeed in English

List your spelling bugs

- **Make a list** of words you regularly misspell. Make a bookmark out of it. Learn them.

- **Learn** these commonly misspelt words:
  all right
  believe
  character
  clothes
  coming
  definite
  friend
  immediately
  receive
  separate

Sob

friend
A freind in need …

Top Tip!

To get full marks in spelling you need to show that you can spell complicated words. So don't just use simple words in your writing.

Beware of homophones

- Some common words **sound the same** but are spelt differently. Learn these and look out for others:

  - *their* (belonging to them), *they're* (= they are), *there* (where)

  - *whose* (belonging to someone), *who's* (= who is)

  - *quiet* (calm), *quite* (a bit)

  - *accept* (take), *except* (apart from)

  - *effect* (noun), *affect* (verb)

whose
Who's clothes are these?

Spot Check

1 Which of these words are spelt incorrectly?
   quitely, responsible, dissapoint, desperate, beleive, friend, weird, neccessary, occasion.
2 What is the difference between *accept* and *except*?
3 Give a mnemonic that helps you spell.

Other spelling tips

- Master a few **spelling rules**.

Pages 58–9.

- Use **mnemonics**, (memory joggers), e.g. Remember there is **iron** in the env**iron**ment, a **rat** in sepa**rat**e, **finite** in de**finite** and a **cog** in re**cog**nise.

- Group words into **families**, e.g. <u>succ</u>ess, <u>succ</u>essful, <u>succ</u>eed; <u>writ</u>ing, <u>writ</u>er, <u>writ</u>ten

- **Say the word** in your mind as it is spelt, e.g. Fe**bru**ary, Wed**nes**day

- Break words into smaller chunks, e.g. *ex-treme-ly, re-le-vant.*

Example

A student has checked this paragraph and corrected the spelling in places. Read the paragraph and the examiner's comment.

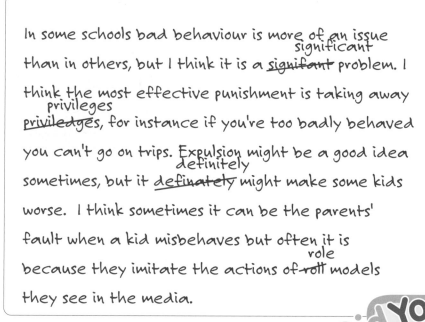

In some schools bad behaviour is more of an issue
than in others, but I think it is a ~~significant~~ problem. I
significant
think the most effective punishment is taking away
privileges
~~priviledges~~, for instance if you've too badly behaved
you can't go on trips. Expulsion might be a good idea
sometimes, but it ~~definately~~ might make some kids
definitely
worse. I think sometimes it can be the parents'
fault when a kid misbehaves but often it is
because they imitate the actions of ~~roll~~ models
role
they see in the media.

Comment

All spelling is correct, including complex and irregular words such as *definitely* and *privileges*. A wide range of vocabulary has been chosen. Therefore 4 marks out of 4 are awarded for spelling.

Did You Know?

The first printers added letters to the ends of words to straighten the right-hand edge of their texts. Spelling wasn't so important in the Middle Ages!

Planning and structure

- You need to plan the **structure** of your story carefully:

  – Give your story an **introduction**, a **development** (build up), a **crisis** and a **resolution** (when things are sorted out).

  – If you want a **fast moving** story, make it exciting and full of tension.

  – If you want a **slow moving** story, focus more on character, feelings and description.

  – Sometimes you are asked to write only the **beginning** of a story.

  – Be daring: *begin* in the middle of the action, then backtrack. Or **end** with a cliffhanger, or a clever twist.

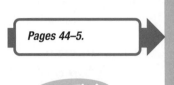

Pages 44–5.

Top Tip!

Before you begin writing, think about how you are going to end your story. This will give the whole story a good structure and purpose.

Characters

- Your characters need to be **believable** and **interesting**. Don't include more than two or three, or they will become just names.

- Describe characters by how they **look**, what they **say** and what they **do**. Often their feelings are better **implied** than stated directly:
  The children felt very cold. ✗
  The children huddled together, their teeth chattering. ✓

- Get **under the skin** of the main character and write from their point of view.

- Keep your **viewpoint consistent**. If you begin writing as the main character (using 'I'), stick to it.

Shiver

Dialogue

- Speech adds **variety** to your story. It also **develops the characters and the plot** and brings both to life.

- Make speech **realistic**. People speak in short sentences and don't always obey the rules of Standard English. Think what *you* would say, and how *you* would say it.

- Follow the rules for **punctuating** speech, and other guidelines.

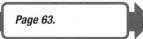

Page 63.

Language

- Make your sentences **interesting**. Think carefully about the words that you use. In particular:

- Use **adjectives** and **adverbs** to give descriptive detail, especially to create the setting.

- Use powerful **nouns** and **verbs** for effect.

- Include some **imagery**.

- **Vary** the length and type of your sentences.

Page 18 (imagery) and pages 48–9 (variety).

Example

Follow these guidelines when writing dialogue.

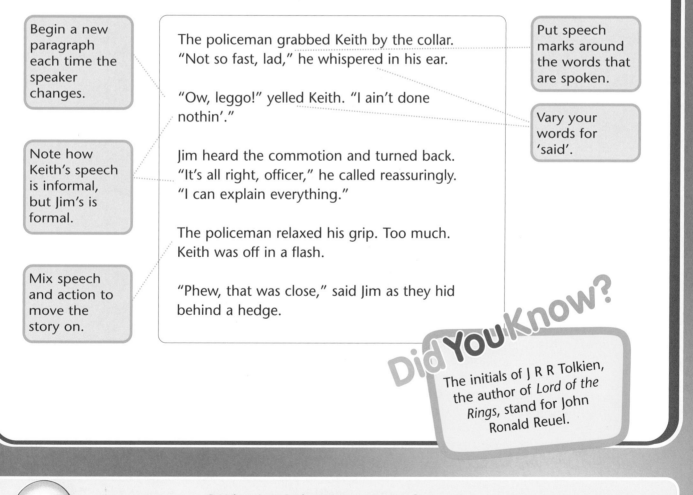

Begin a new paragraph each time the speaker changes.

Note how Keith's speech is informal, but Jim's is formal.

Mix speech and action to move the story on.

Put speech marks around the words that are spoken.

Vary your words for 'said'.

The policeman grabbed Keith by the collar. "Not so fast, lad," he whispered in his ear.

"Ow, leggo!" yelled Keith. "I ain't done nothin'."

Jim heard the commotion and turned back. "It's all right, officer," he called reassuringly. "I can explain everything."

The policeman relaxed his grip. Too much. Keith was off in a flash.

"Phew, that was close," said Jim as they hid behind a hedge.

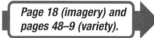

Did You Know?

The initials of J R R Tolkien, the author of *Lord of the Rings*, stand for John Ronald Reuel.

Spot Check

1 What is a 3rd person narrative?
2 'The more characters the better.' True or false?
3 What is the difference between an unfinished story and a cliffhanger ending?
4 Give three rules to follow when including dialogue.

Writing to describe

Descriptive writing

- You may be asked to describe an **event**, **place** or **person**. Your aim is to tell the readers about it in an interesting and entertaining way.

- Descriptions mean giving more than the facts. You have to **bring the event, person or place to life** by using language effectively.

- The description does not have to be true, but it has to be **believable**.

Planning and structure

- If this is the longer writing task, use the planning grid provided.

- A **spider diagram** is good for planning description. Brainstorm **different ideas** on the subject. Then decide on the **order**.

- Start with the main idea in the middle and branch out like this:

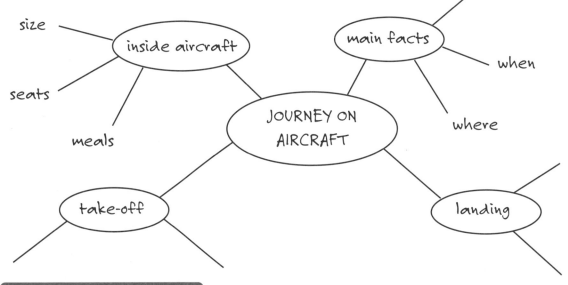

Descriptive language

- Use the **senses**. Describe what you see, so that others can see it. But also what you smell, hear, touch, taste and feel, e.g.
  I jumped as the elephant lifted its trunk and bellowed.

- Use **powerful words**, especially nouns, verbs and adjectives. Replace dull words with interesting ones, e.g.
  The town ~~was full of~~ rang with the cries of street sellers.

- Include some special **imagery** if you can (similes, metaphors, etc), e.g. *His eyebrows scuttled like spiders across his brow.*

- Go into **detail**. Precise description is more powerful than general comments, e.g.
  I put on my ~~hat~~ thick green bobble hat and opened the door.

- **Vary** the length and type of your sentences.

> **Top Tip!**
>
> You can use these descriptive techniques in other kinds of writing too, especially writing stories.

Pages 48–9.

This is the beginning of a level 7 description of 'a memorable journey'.

level
7

My first trip on an aeroplane, when I was about six, sticks in my mind. Not because it was dramatic in any obvious way – we were going on holiday to Spain, just like millions of other people – but because it was such a new experience for me.

Everything was strange. Even before we boarded I was transfixed by the vast halls full of people, the suitcases disappearing behind the flaps, as if they were being eaten by a mechanical monster, the brisk uniformed officials who always knew where they were going.

The aircraft itself was rather disappointing: I felt like I had moved from a mansion to a broom cupboard. But as soon as the engines whined and the plane lumbered into position, I was gripped again. Take-off was a punch in the chest, which left me breathless. Out of the window I could see London becoming toytown below me.

- Structure is careful and clear. 1st paragraph gives the background.
- Note the long, well-worked sentence.

- Emphasis on writer's feeling – overwhelmed.
- Powerful words: 'transfixed', 'vast'.
- Simile of monster.
- Good contrast between short and long sentence.

- Effective images: 'mansion', 'punch in the chest', 'toytown'.
- Powerful verbs: 'whined', 'lumbered'.
- Emphasis on seeing and feeling.

Did You Know?

A cliché is a phrase that has been over-used, which makes it dull and lifeless. Examples are 'take the bull by the horns' and 'a blessing in disguise'.

Spot Check

1 Give two reasons why a spider diagram is useful for planning descriptions.
2 Does all the description have to be true?
3 Why are adjectives useful in descriptive writing?
4 What is imagery?

WRITING — Writing to inform and explain

Structure and planning

- Spider diagrams are useful planning tools when writing **information**. They allow you to brainstorm ideas and group them by topic.

Page 64.

- **Explanation** texts follow a logical structure. A step-by-step planning tool works well, e.g.

Introduction ⟶ Step 1 ⟶ Step 2

- Use **paragraphs** to organise your writing – one paragraph for each bubble on the diagram.

- Use **connectives** to guide the reader through the text and link the paragraphs, e.g. *first, then, in addition, for example, because, as a result, when, therefore.*

- Begin with a clear **introduction**. You can end with a summary.

- Longer information texts may need **subheadings** or **bullet points**.

Content and language

- Information and explanation texts are are fact-based. They need to be clear and concise. Avoid persuasive or highly descriptive language.

- Use **formal** English, in the **3rd person** (unless the facts are about you):
  I hang out in a youth club, but there's another one too. ✗
  Teenagers have the choice of two youth clubs. ✓

Pages 42 and 46.

Top Tip!

Remember your **audience** when writing. Children will need a different approach to (say) parents or older people.

- Begin each paragraph with a **general statement** (topic sentence), then continue with further **detail** or **examples**, e.g.
  Animals can do some extraordinary things. Pumas, for example, can jump up to 20 metres.

- If you are writing a **newspaper report**, include the main facts in the first one or two paragraphs, then fill out background detail later; include quotes and a snappy headline.

Pages 50–1.

This is an extract from a level 7 information sheet, written by a student about their own house, for a 'time capsule'.

level
7

Built in the 1890s from Cotswold stone, the house is attached to both its neighbours, forming a terrace of three. However, there is plenty of space for a family of five, as it is spread over four floors.

The ground floor consists of a small entrance hall which leads to a double-sized living room with an open fire, piano and hi-fi. At one end is a large, kitchen extension; at the other is a south-facing conservatory with a sofa and TV. There is also a downstairs toilet.

On the first floor is a large single bedroom and a bathroom with a walk-in shower. There are two bedrooms on the second floor, one of which is double. At the very top of the house is a converted attic bedroom with a large window in the roof. Three of the bedrooms have fantastic views across the valley; on a clear day you can even see the Black Mountains in Wales.

Language:
– clear and factual – lots of nouns
– consistently written in 3rd person – no 'me' or 'our'
– good range of sentence types to keep interest
– formal English throughout

Structure:
– well-organised, with one topic per paragraph
– topic sentences make it clear what the topic is
– connectives guide the reader, e.g. 'however', 'also'

Did You Know?

English borrows from many other languages, e.g. *hamburger* (German), *kayak* (Eskimo) and *shampoo* (Hindi).

Spot Check

1 'The main aim of an information text is to entertain the reader.' True or false?
2 Why is a step-by-step planning tool useful for explanation texts?
3 What kind of connectives would you expect to include in an explanation text?
4 Give two special features of news reports.

Writing to discuss and review

Structure and planning

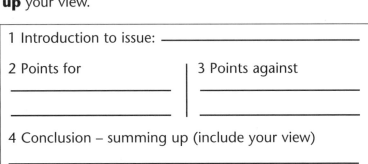

- A spider diagram is a useful planning tool for a **review**. Give each feature of the book, film, etc. a different bubble, e.g.
  – for a **book**: plot, characters, language, themes
  – for a **film**: plot, acting, special effects, direction

  Page 64.

- Begin with **information** about the product, then **one paragraph per feature**, then **sum up** your view.

- Use the planning tool on the right for a balanced **discussion**.

- Use **connectives** to guide the reader through the discussion, e.g. *therefore, in addition, on the other hand, however.*

- Make it clear **who holds what views**, e.g. *Other people say …, Opponents argue …*

1 Introduction to issue: ——————————
2 Points for	3 Points against
————————	————————
————————	————————
4 Conclusion – summing up (include your view)
————————————————

Language and style

- In **discussion** texts:

  – use **formal** language, e.g. *A view shared by many is that …*

  – give **examples** and **quote** people's views, e.g.
  Sandra, for example, says, 'Smokers should pay for their own hospital bills.' (direct speech)
  Sandra believes that smokers should pay for their own hospital bills. (indirect speech)

  – present people's views **fairly** – put your own view in the **conclusion**.

SMOKERS SHOULD PAY FOR THEIR OWN HOSPITAL BILLS.

- In **reviews**:

  – the purpose is to **entertain** as well as **inform**, so your style can be more **lively** and **informal**, e.g.
  Flip to the end and you'll get a shock.

  – cover both the **good and bad points** of the product.

  – include your **own view** throughout, e.g. *I felt that …*

  – write in the **present tense**, e.g. *The special effects are amazing, the characters fail to convince.*

  Pages 47 and 49 (reviews).

This is the start of a discussion which analyses the results of a survey on attitudes to single-sex schools.

Choosing between a single-sex or a mixed school can be quite a dilemma for students as well as parents. And both groups of people are deeply divided on the issue, as the survey shows.

Those who favour single-sex schools, like Louise, often say that they allow students to learn, without getting distracted by romantic attachments. But opponents like Rob argue that most schools in the country are mixed, and plenty of learning goes on in them.

Whether single-sex schools are 'natural' is another issue. Several students think that all-boy or all-girl classes don't reflect real-life situations. However, others, such as Yajnah, point out that schools are unnatural anyway.

Top Tip!

When planning a discussion, instead of grouping all the points 'for' together, followed by all the points 'against', you may like to take each point at a time and explore the views for and against. This approach has been taken in the example here.

Structure:
– clear introduction to the issue
– one paragraph for each point
– good use of connectives to guide reader, eg 'however', 'but opponents …'

Language/style:
– formal language throughout
– balanced approach which doesn't show writer's view
– refers to people's views in detail

Did YOU Know?

When *Coronation Street* first hit the TV screens in 1960, the *Daily Mirror* reviewer said, 'I find it hard to believe that viewers will want to put up with a continuous slice of domestic drudgery two evenings a week.' How wrong he was!

Spot Check

1 Which is usually written in more formal language, a discussion or a review?
2 How can you make the structure of a discussion balanced?
3 'You shouldn't include your own opinion in a review.' True or false?
4 Give three connectives that could be useful in a discussion.

Writing to persuade, argue, advise

Structure and planning

- Persuasive writing usually consists of a **series of points** in a **logical order**. This is a useful planning tool:

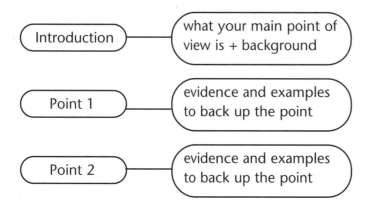

Introduction	what your main point of view is + background
Point 1	evidence and examples to back up the point
Point 2	evidence and examples to back up the point

- Give each point a **new paragraph**.

- Begin with an **introduction** and end with a powerful **conclusion**.

- **Connectives** are important to join up your ideas, e.g. *therefore, because, firstly*.

Language and style

- If you are writing an argument, you may want to sound **reasonable** (think about the purpose and audience of the task). Use **formal language** and avoid exaggerating.

- Think of your **opponent's arguments** and try to counter them.

- Include some **rhetorical techniques**, e.g.

  – **emotive words**: *starving* (not *hungry*), *children* (not *people*)

  – **repetition**: *it isn't fair and it isn't just*

  – **alliteration**: *a **pr**essing **pr**oblem*

  – **rhetorical questions** (where the answer is obvious): *Are we to take this seriously?*

  – **personal pronouns**: *we* includes the audience, *you* addresses the audience directly

- For **more persuasive** writing, such as a speech encouraging a sports team, include more rhetorical techniques!

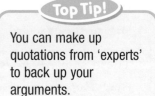

- When **writing to advise**:

  – Use softer language and a friendly tone, e.g.
  Have you thought about …?

  – Include words like *should, could, may* and *perhaps* to make suggestions.

  – Informal language may be appropriate, depending on the audience, e.g. *Check this out!*

  – Give reasons why your advice should be followed, e.g.
  If you do this, then …

Page 51 (advice texts).

Example

Here is a level 7 piece of writing arguing against banning access to the Internet.

level
7

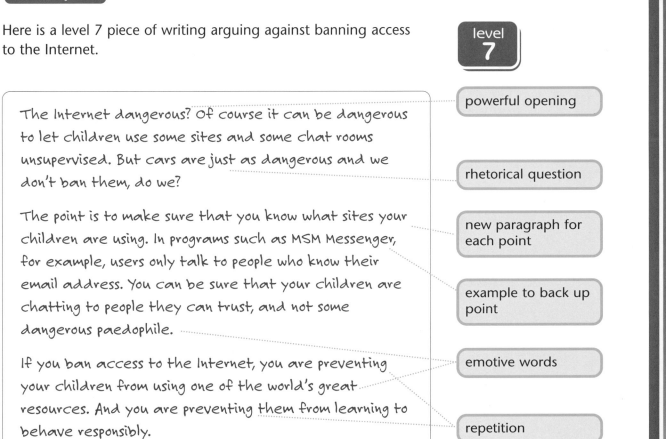

The Internet dangerous? Of course it can be dangerous to let children use some sites and some chat rooms unsupervised. But cars are just as dangerous and we don't ban them, do we?

The point is to make sure that you know what sites your children are using. In programs such as MSM Messenger, for example, users only talk to people who know their email address. You can be sure that your children are chatting to people they can trust, and not some dangerous paedophile.

If you ban access to the Internet, you are preventing your children from using one of the world's great resources. And you are preventing them from learning to behave responsibly.

- powerful opening
- rhetorical question
- new paragraph for each point
- example to back up point
- emotive words
- repetition

Spot Check

1 How do paragraphs help you structure an argument?
2 Give three rhetorical techniques.
3 Which of these adjectives would you avoid in persuasive writing?
   fantastic, wonderful, amazing, good, excellent
4 In what kind of writing are you likely to use words like *would, should* and *may?*

WRITING   Raising your level

Follow these guidelines to improve your writing from level 6 to level 7.

Structure and organisation

- **Structure** your writing for maximum impact. Make your **introduction** and **conclusion** really count – use a dramatic beginning or surprising ending in a story, for example.

- Make the structure of any argument or discussion crystal clear by using **paragraphs** and **connectives**.

- **Develop** and link the points within each paragraph.

Content

- In **stories**, make sure your characters and dialogue are **believable**.

- In non-fiction, **brainstorm** interesting, thoughtful ideas before you start writing.

Audience and purpose

- Take **audience** and **purpose** into account at all times, e.g.

  – keep up the same level of **formality** that the task demands

  – choose a distinctive **voice** and stick to it throughout.

Language

- Make every word count.

- Use different **sentence structures** for emphasis and variety.

- Use language for **special effects**, e.g. to create tension in a story.

- Make full use of **rhetorical techniques** in persuasive writing.

Top Tip!

Give yourself enough checking time – this is where you can pick up those extra marks.

Punctuation, grammar and spelling

- Use the **full range of punctuation** accurately to structure your sentences and make the meaning clear.

- Make sure there are **no grammatical errors**.

- **Spell** all your words **correctly**, including complex words.

Remember to practise spelling!

Example

Read this level 6 piece of writing, intended to advise students on good study skills. The notes show how it could be raised to a level 7.

How NOT to study

Do you want to make the **worst** use of your time when you get down to work? Then simply follow this advice...

- **Don't get into a study routine.** If you find you are developing a routine, such as studying as soon as you get home from school, then **don't**. Routines only make it easier to start work. So make sure you don't develop any helpful working habits like this.

- **Work non-stop.** Regular breaks actually increase your work out put because you return to work refreshed. So keep your nose to your desk for at least three hours at a time, and you will see the benefits, boredom and tiredness.

- **Don't get distracted.** A noisy place is a disaster if you want to study effectiveley. So avoid doing your studying on the bus, or in the television room with your mobile switched on. The interuptions will seriously distract you from doing any proper work.

A clever idea to turn the advice round like this, but the final paragraph needs to keep the irony up.

Use of words is usually effective, but 'don't' here is dull and repetitive – replace it with 'cut it out'.

Some incorrect spelling loses the student marks: 'output', 'effectively', 'interruption'.

More variety in punctuation needed, e.g. use a dash here instead of a comma.

Paragraphs and bullets used to good effect, but piece needs a good conclusion.

Shakespeare's plays are an essential part of the Key Stage 3 (and Key Stage 4) curriculum but students often get a bit stressed about studying his work because it can seem complicated when you first start to read it. Don't panic! Your teacher and this book will see you through and not only will you understand what is happening, you'll even enjoy the play and find yourself wondering which one you'll study at Key Stage 4. This book mainly draws examples from two famous plays, *The Tempest* and *Romeo and Juliet*.

Top tips when starting Shakespeare

- Give it a go and try to read the **words aloud** – they might look strange on the page but will often make sense when you hear them.

- Try to see the play on **stage** or **screen**, or, better still, have a go yourself!

- Try to **remember** who the **characters** are. Some of the characters can have strange or unfamiliar names so draw a family tree or cut out faces for each of the characters so you can remember who says what.

- Pull out the **words** and **phrases** that you especially like – you could make them into a poster with key images on them.

- If the plot gets complicated (and it often does) try making a **plot diagram** to keep track of what is happening.

- Try to have fun – there are often really funny bits in every play. Watch out for them!

Key areas to consider

You will be asked a question about **one** of these four aspects of the play:

- **Character and motivation** – who the main characters are and why they behave as they do.

  Pages 84–5.

- **Ideas, themes and issues** – the key ideas the play explores and makes you think about.

  Pages 86–7.

- **Language** – what the characters say and the impact this is intended to and does have on the audience.

  Pages 78–9 and 88–9.

- **Performance** – how the play works on stage and how the audience responds to it. Think about how you might put on the play if you were the director.

  Pages 90–1.

Your teacher might give you a practice question like this. The labels show you how easy it is to break down a question before you start planning your answer.

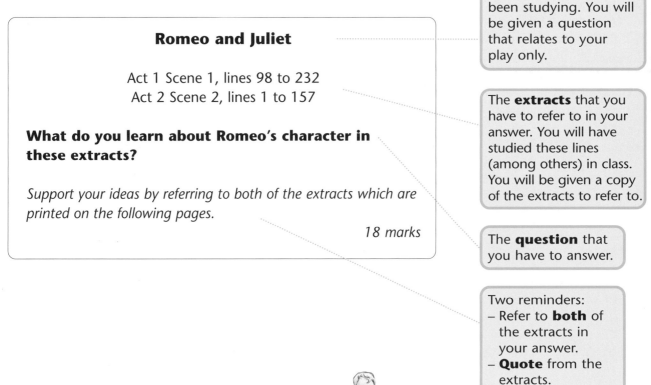

Romeo and Juliet

Act 1 Scene 1, lines 98 to 232
Act 2 Scene 2, lines 1 to 157

What do you learn about Romeo's character in these extracts?

Support your ideas by referring to both of the extracts which are printed on the following pages.

18 marks

The **play** you have been studying. You will be given a question that relates to your play only.

The **extracts** that you have to refer to in your answer. You will have studied these lines (among others) in class. You will be given a copy of the extracts to refer to.

The **question** that you have to answer.

Two reminders:
– Refer to **both** of the extracts in your answer.
– **Quote** from the extracts.

Did You Know?

There have been over 400 films made of Shakespeare's plays.

Spot Check

True or false?
1 You only have to study one Shakespeare play.
2 You are assessed on your historical knowledge about Shakespeare's life and times.
3 It helps to think about how the play could be performed.
4 You should spend 10 minutes planning your answer.

Shakespeare's plays

Tragedy, comedy, history, romance

Shakespeare wrote different kinds of plays:

- **Tragedies** are serious and end with the main character's death. They explore power, jealousy, ambition and love. Examples: *Macbeth, Romeo and Juliet.*

- **Comedies** are light-hearted and have a happy ending. They explore the relationships of men and women in love, and include misunderstandings and disguise. Examples: *Much Ado About Nothing, As You Like It.*

- **Histories** tell the story of English kings. They explore conflict, loyalty and what it means to be a king. Examples: *Richard III, Henry V.*

- **Romances** begin tragically and end happily. They are sometimes called 'tragicomedies'. Examples: *The Tempest, Pericles.*

Shakespeare's world

William Shakespeare (born 1564, died 1616) lived during the reigns of Elizabeth I and James I. The world was very different then:

- **Kings and queens** were all-powerful. People believed they were chosen by God to rule the country.

- The **upper classes** (nobles, e.g. dukes) also had a lot of power. The **lower classes** (ordinary people) had to respect their superiors.

- There was a lot of **political conflict**, including plots against the rulers.

- **Men** had far more power than women.

- People were very **religious** and **superstitious**. They believed in witches and magic.

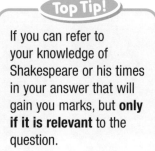

Top Tip!

If you can refer to your knowledge of Shakespeare or his times in your answer that will gain you marks, but **only if it is relevant** to the question.

The theatre

- The theatre was very **popular** in Shakespeare's day – people had no TV or cinema. All classes of society watched his plays.

- **Stage** and **scenery** were very simple. There were many rough and ready outdoor productions.

- **Masques** (masked balls) were very popular in the reign of James I. They included music, dance, song and 'special effects'. *The Tempest* has masque-like features.

- Plays are divided into **acts** (large sections) and **scenes** (subsections marking a new time or place). They include dialogue and stage directions.

Example

This extract from *The Tempest*, Act 5 Scene 1, shows some of the issues that were important in Shakespeare's day.

PROSPERO But you, my brace of lords, were I so minded,
              I here could pluck his highness' frown upon you,
              And justify you traitors: at this time
              I will tell no tales.
SEBASTIAN [*Aside*] The devil speaks in him.
PROSPERO   No.
              For you, most wicked sir, whom to call brother
              Would even infect my mouth, I do forgive
              Thy rankest fault; all of them; and require
              My dukedom of thee, which, perforce, I know,
              Thou must restore.

Lords and ladies were key figures in Shakespeare's day, and in his plays.

Treachery – plotting against the crown – was a real issue in the politics of the day.

Everyone believed in **God** and the **Devil**, and thought that there were good and evil spirits.

The plays often end by restoring power to the **rightful ruler**. What made a true ruler was a question much debated.

Did You Know?

Women were not allowed to act in Shakespeare's day, so boys played all the female roles.

Spot Check

1 Why did Shakespeare write about kings?
2 Give two differences between the theatre in Shakespeare's time and today.
3 Give two features of Shakespeare's comedies.

Different kinds of language

- Most of the lines are in **blank verse** (unrhymed poetry). Each line has a regular pattern of **10 syllables**, with emphasis on every other syllable:
  Go, <u>charge</u> my <u>gob</u>lins <u>that</u> they <u>grind</u> their <u>joints</u>

- Some passages are in **prose** (ordinary writing), especially when comic characters and the lower classes are speaking: *What have we here? a man or a fish? dead or alive? A fish: he smells like a fish …*

- **Long speeches** are often full of expression and feeling. **Soliloquies** (speeches when the actor is alone on stage) show the audience what the character is thinking and feeling.

- Characters often speak **alternate lines** when tense or arguing, e.g.

GREGORY	Do you quarrel, sir?
ABRAHAM	Quarrel sir! no, sir.
SAMPSON	If you do, sir, I am for you: I serve as good a man as you.
ABRAHAM	No better.

Top Tip!

Reading the script aloud, slowly, will help you to understand it. Do not pause at the end of the lines unless there is a comma or full stop.

Expressive language

- Shakespeare uses **striking vocabulary** (choice of words):
  - to convey a character's **feelings**, e.g. *To fleer and scorn at our solemnity* (Tybalt saying what he thinks Romeo intends to do, in *Romeo and Juliet*).
  - to draw a vivid **picture**, e.g. *plunged in the foaming brine* (Ariel about the shipwreck, in *The Tempest*).

- He also uses **word play**, especially in comic scenes:
  Though thou canst swim like a duck, thou art made like a goose (Stephano about Trinculo, in *The Tempest*).

- **Sound effects** such as **alliteration** (repeated sounds) add power to the poetry, e.g. *… the bark thy body is, Sailing in this salt flood; the winds, thy sighs* (*Romeo and Juliet*).

- Shakespeare uses **imagery** to draw word pictures in the minds of the audience:
  - **similes**: *Like a rich jewel in Ethiope's ear* (Romeo describing Juliet in *Romeo and Juliet*)
  - **metaphors**: *My lips, two blushing pilgrims, ready stand* (Romeo in *Romeo and Juliet*)
  - **personification**: *The winds did sing it to me, and the thunder* (*The Tempest*)

Unfamiliar features

Shakespeare's language is 400 years old and highly poetic. Look out for these features:

- **old-fashioned words**, e.g. *thee/thou* (= you), *thy* (= your), *hath/hast* (= has)

- **strange word order**, e.g. *Thee of thy son, Alonso, they have bereft* (= They have taken your son away from you, Alonso.)

- **missing letters**, e.g. *'scape* = escape, *shak'd* = shaked (shook). Note that *shak'd* is pronounced as one syllable, *shaked* as two syllables.

Example

The spirit Ariel describes how he casts a spell on the drunken Caliban and his friends (*The Tempest*, Act 4 Scene 1). Note:
- the **similes** – he compares them first to young horses (colts), then to calves following the sound of the mooing of the herd
- the **vivid description** of the scene.

> Then I beat my tabor*,
> At which, like unback'd* colts, they prick'd their ears,
> Advanc'd their eyelids, lifted up their noses
> As they smelt music: so I charm'd their ears
> That, calf-like, they my lowing* follow'd through
> Tooth'd briers, sharp furzes, pricking goss and thorns,
> Which enter'd their frail shins: at last I left them
> I' the filthy-mantled* pool beyond your cell,
> There dancing up to the chins, that the foul lake
> O'erstunk their feet.

*drum

*not yet ridden

*mooing

*refers to the stagnant 'coat' on the pool

Spot Check

1 What does 'blank verse' mean?
2 When does Shakespeare use prose?
3 What is alliteration?
4 What two types of imagery are used in this quote from *The Tempest*?
   their great guilt, like poison given to work a great time after, now 'gins to bite the spirits

Understand the question

To give a precise and relevant answer you need to think carefully about what the question is asking you to do. Look at these questions, for example:

> How does Caliban's language show his feelings for Prospero?

This question is about Shakespeare's **language**. The focus is on **Caliban's feelings** for Prospero, in *The Tempest*.

> What problems would the director have to solve in putting on these scenes?

The question is about **performing** the play. The focus is on **problems** in performance.

> What different impressions of Romeo do we get in these extracts?

The question is about the **character** of Romeo. The focus is on the **different sides** of his character, including **why** he behaves as he does (his motivation).

> **Top Tip!**
>
> Your essay needs to be **balanced**, so make sure you cover **all the scenes** in your planning.

Re-read the extracts

- You should read the extracts again, with the question in mind.

- **Highlight the key words** or passages that relate to the question.

- Add any short **notes** in the margin that occur to you as you read.

Brainstorm ideas

- Jot down some **key words** or **ideas**, and add some **thoughts** and **quotations** next to them. Use a spider diagram or other planning tool to help you, as in the plan for this question about *Romeo and Juliet*:

What impressions do we get of Romeo in these extracts?

'Ay me, sad hours seem long' — melancholy lover

Impressions of Romeo

indifferent to family loyalty — 'My name ... is hateful to myself'

has switched affections from Rosaline to Juliet — different in 2nd extract

passionate and brave now — '... thy kinsmen are no stop to me'

- Use this as the **plan** for your answer.

- Decide on the **order** in which you will discuss each main point. **Number** them on your plan.

Here is a completed plan to answer the question:

What impression do we get of Romeo in Act 1 Scene 1 and Act 2 Scene 2?

Intro	– both scenes are key for R's character
Act 1 Scene 1	
melancholy	– 'Ay me, sad hours seem long'
in love	– 'I do love a woman'
in turmoil	– 'cold fire, sick health'
warm friend	– 'Good heart' (to Benvolio)
witty	– 'A right good mark-man!'
Act 2 Scene 2	
in love	– 'It is my lady! – O, it is my love!'
romantic	– 'O that I were a glove upon that hand'
not proud	– 'My name, dear saint, is hateful to myself'
brave	– 'thy kinsmen are no stop to me'
witty	– '... love from love, toward school with heavy looks'
Conclusion	– moping at first, but boldly passionate about Juliet

Did You Know?

The 'Reduced Shakespeare' theatre company have summarised all 37 of Shakespeare's plays and turned them into one fast-moving comedy lasting an hour and a half.

- Note that this plan takes **each scene** in turn.

- If you are confident, you could take **each impression** of Romeo in turn, and discuss how he appears romantic, clever, etc. in both scenes:

Intro – both scenes are key for R's character. Moping in first, passionate in second.
Lover: 'I do love a woman' (Act 1); 'O, it is my love!' (Act 2)
Witty: 'A right good mark-man!' (Act 1); ... toward school with heavy looks'

- This approach is more difficult to follow, but is more focused and impressive when you carry it off.

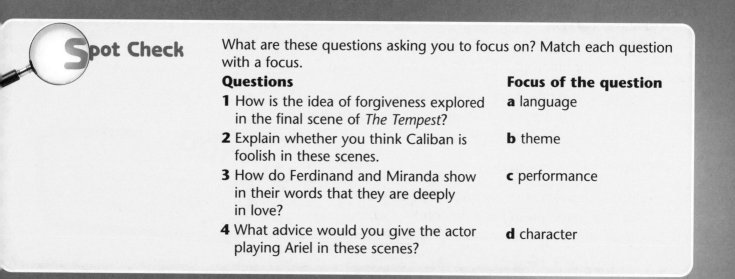

Spot Check

What are these questions asking you to focus on? Match each question with a focus.

Questions

1 How is the idea of forgiveness explored in the final scene of *The Tempest*?

2 Explain whether you think Caliban is foolish in these scenes.

3 How do Ferdinand and Miranda show in their words that they are deeply in love?

4 What advice would you give the actor playing Ariel in these scenes?

Focus of the question

a language

b theme

c performance

d character

Begin and end effectively

- Begin with an **introduction**. This should:
  - show that you **understand the question**, without giving a detailed answer.
  - refer to the **key words** in the question, e.g. *Romeo's language* or *Caliban's feelings*.
  - refer to the **context**, e.g. *in these scenes* or *in Act 1 Scene 3*

- The final paragraph should be a **conclusion**. This should:
  - return to the **focus** of the question, e.g. *Romeo's language, therefore, …*
  - draw together the **key points**, e.g. *We have seen that Caliban's feelings are wide-ranging: first he is …*

Refer to the extracts

- Often you can **summarise** or **paraphrase** the evidence. This means using your own words, e.g. *Antonio suggests a brutal plot to murder the sleeping king.*

- You also need to **quote directly** from the extracts. This helps you make your point, and shows the examiners that you understand the play. Use **inverted commas** to show you are quoting.

- You can embed **short quotations** in your sentences, e.g. *In a powerful image, Ariel describes Ferdinand's hair as standing up 'like reeds'.*

- **Longer quotations** should start a new line, and be indented. Keep them as short as you can but still make your point.

- Remember: **Point – Evidence – Comment**. Begin by making your own point, in your own words. Then quote from the extract to back up your point. Finally, use your own words to explain how the quotation backs up your point.

Top Tip!

For each main point that you make in your answer, give a quotation from the extracts and explain why it is relevant.

Page 83.

Write well

- **Write clearly**. Use one paragraph per point. Use connectives to link your ideas, e.g. *in addition, by contrast, also, however.*

- **Write with style.** Make your answer stand out from the others. Think of interesting words to use, vary your sentence structure and be bold in expressing your opinion.

- Keep your tone **formal**.

- Don't just give a brief discussion of each point – **develop your points** in a thoughtful and convincing way so that your answer thoroughly **analyses** the issue.

Did You Know?

You can rearrange the letters in 'William Shakespeare' to make 'I am a weakish speller'.

This is the beginning of an answer to the question:

How does Shakespeare make the audience laugh in Act 2 Scene 2 and Act 3 Scene 2 of *The Tempest*?

level
6

Shakespeare uses all sorts of skills in these scenes to make the audience laugh. His characters are amusing, the language they use is funny, and there is a lot of slapstick and misunderstanding.

At the beginning of the first extract Caliban thinks that Trinculo is a spirit sent by Prospero to torment him. This is deliberately funny, as Trinculo is only a jester. Shakespeare could have cleared the misunderstanding up very quickly by making Caliban realise that Trinculo is not a spirit, but he keeps the idea going for a long time. When Stephano sings his song, Caliban yells 'Do not torment me: O!' and he repeats this after Stephano's next speech. Each time Caliban makes this mistake, the audience will roar with laughter.

Introduction:
– Refers to the key words in the question ('make the audience laugh').
– Refers to the context ('these scenes').
– Gives a summary of the key points, which will be developed in the answer.

Reference to the extract without using a quotation, but still with a comment.

Point – misunderstanding is kept going.
Evidence – 'Do not torment me: O!'
Comment – why it is effective.

Answer is **well organised** (one paragraph for the first main point), **clear** and **well written**.

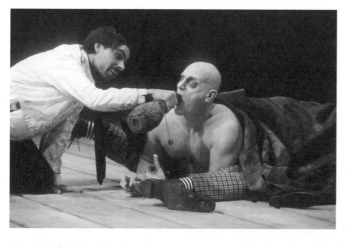

Stephano forces Caliban to drink while Trinculo hides under the covers (from Act 2 Scene 2, *The Tempest*). This photograph is from a modern interpretation performed by the Royal Shakespeare Company.

Spot Check

1 Give two things that an introduction should do.
2 Why should you quote directly from the extracts?
3 What does 'Point – Evidence – Comment' help you to remember?
4 What are these connectives useful for?
   in the same way, similarly, too, also

Answering questions on characters

Revising for questions on characters

You may be asked to describe how a character behaves in the set scenes, or what is going on in a relationship. In order to prepare for a question like this:

- **Draw up a character log** for the characters in your play, with brief descriptions of who they are. Some of this could be in the form of a diagram showing connections, e.g.

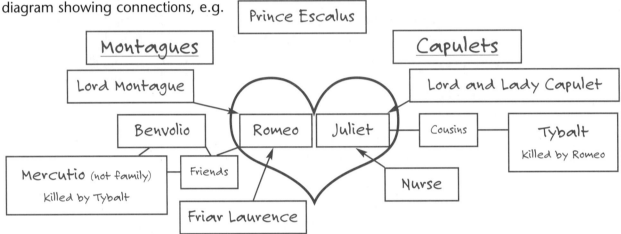

- Take two or three of the main characters and compile a **spider diagram of their key qualities**, e.g.

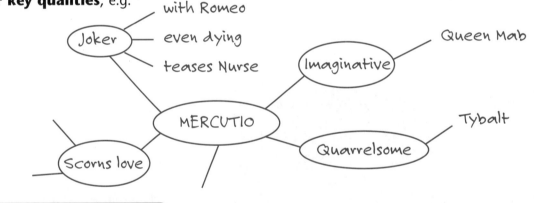

Describing a character

When describing what a character is like, refer to:

- **what they say**, e.g. *Caliban acts like a slave. He says, 'I will kiss thy foot.'*

- **what they do**, e.g. *Caliban shows Prospero 'all the qualities o' th' isle'.*

- **what others say** about them, e.g. *Trinculo calls him 'a most ridiculous monster'.*

- **why they behave** as they do (their motivation), e.g. *Caliban wanted to kill Prospero so that he could live on his island as a free man.*

Top Tip!
Whenever you make a point about a character, back it up with a quote from the extracts.

Remember that characters can **change** in the course of the play, e.g. Richard loses control of events the more that he plots and kills, in *Richard III*.

Writing in role

Occasionally you are asked to write as if you were one of the characters of the play. This means you have to:

- get under the skin of your character, by **imagining what it feels** like to be them in that situation.

- **stay in role** – refer to yourself throughout as 'I' and 'me' and keep that pretence going.

- **explain** what you are doing, thinking and feeling and why (your motivation).

- **quote** from the set scenes to back up what you say.

Example

This is the start of a level 7 answer to the question:

What impression do we get of Capulet in Act 1 Scene 2 and Act 3 Scene 5 of *Romeo and Juliet*?

level 7

Although Capulet gives the impression of being a strong character in both scenes, his attitude towards Juliet is very different.

> Good introduction: summarises the answer and uses the key word 'impression'.

In the first scene Capulet appears to be a concerned and loving father. When Paris asks if he can marry Juliet, Capulet says she is too young: 'My child is yet a stranger in the world'. When Paris argues that other girls marry younger, Capulet rejects this: 'And too soon marr'd are those so early made.' As his only child, 'She is the hopeful lady of my earth.'

> Commenting on what Capulet does.

> Commenting on what Capulet says.

> Commenting on why he behaves as he does.

Capulet, however, takes the traditional authoritarian role in the second scene. He cannot believe that she is refusing to obey him when he has found her a good husband. He is so angry that he threatens to throw her out:

> A new paragraph for the new point.

An you be mine, I'll give you to my friend;
And you be not, hang, beg, starve, die in the streets.

> Quotations are well chosen and carefully included in the answer.

This shows that he regards Juliet as his possession.

Spot Check   Choose two of the main characters in your play. Draw up a spider diagram for each one, to display their key features or qualities.

Answering questions on ideas and themes

Knowing the story

- You won't be asked to discuss the **plot** (the story of the whole play), but you do need to know about the **key events** to understand the play and how the extracts fit in to the whole.

- Draw up a **storyline** to remind yourself of the plot, like this one about *The Tempest*:

> Act 1   The shipwreck
>
>   Prospero tells Miranda about his past
>
>   The history of the spirit Ariel is described
>
>   Prospero and Miranda visit Caliban

Did You Know?

William Shakespeare was the first person to refer to a coward as 'chicken'.

Top Tip!

If you are asked about a theme, relate it to the scenes provided. Remember to back up your ideas with quotes from the extracts.

Themes

Themes are the **main ideas** explored in a play:

The Tempest
- **forgiveness** – Prospero and his enemies, Caliban and Prospero
- **civilisation** – the 'savage' Caliban compared with the 'civilised' dukes
- **master and servant** – Caliban/Ariel and Prospero, Gonzalo and Alonso
- **magic** – Prospero a 'good' magician, Ariel a spirit
- **love and marriage** – Miranda and Ferdinand, tested by Prospero
- **parenthood** – Prospero and Miranda, Alonso and Ferdinand
- **nature v. nurture** – Prospero tries to civilise Caliban, but fails

Romeo and Juliet
- **destiny** – 'star-crossed lovers', Romeo's apprehension, undelivered letter
- **love and marriage** – Romeo and Juliet (and Rosaline), Paris
- **hate** – two families, Tybalt
- **parenthood** – Capulet and Juliet, Lady Capulet v. Nurse, Montague
- **death** – Mercutio, Tybalt, Romeo, Juliet, Paris, Capulet vault
- **friendship** – Romeo, Mercutio, Benvolio, also in a sense Friar and Romeo

Preparing for a question on theme

- Draw up a spider diagram for each theme of your play. Add detail as you study it, e.g.

Prospero a 'good' witch – uses powers to serve good

brings Ferdinand and Miranda together

arranges for a reconciliation with Antonio

Magic in 'The Tempest'

Caliban's mother Sycorax a 'bad' witch

Ariel a spirit with magic powers

Context – people believed in magic –James I wrote about witchcraft

Example

This is the start of a level 7 answer to the question:

What different ideas about love and marriage are explored in Act 3 Scene 4 and Act 3 Scene 5 of *Romeo and Juliet*?

level 7

In these scenes Shakespeare contrasts opposing ideas about love and marriage: the tradition of arranged marriage and the passion of love at first sight.

In the first scene Paris observes the rules of courtship, coming to woo Juliet and win her love. Her father had intended to ask her if she would like to marry Paris, but there has been 'no time to move our daughter'. Nonetheless, he now assumes that she will do what he tells her to do: 'I think she will be ruled in all respects by me'.

This is the traditional Elizabethan assumption – that a daughter obeyed her father. Capulet seems to want to get Juliet married off as soon as possible, as if it is a business arrangement:

'o' Thursday, tell her,
She shall be married to this noble earl.'

Paris is a good match and Capulet doesn't want to lose him. This practical attitude is compared with the romance of the second scene, in which the lovers cannot bear to part.

Good **introduction**: summarises the answer and uses the key words 'ideas about love and marriage'.

'In the first scene' and 'Nonetheless' help to **organise** and '**signpost**' the answer.

Quotations are well chosen and carefully included in the answer.

Note **Point – Evidence – Comment**.

Throughout the focus is on **ideas about love and marriage** in the **two** scenes given.

Spot Check

Choose two of the main themes of your play. Draw up a spider diagram for each one, showing how the theme is explored in different scenes and by different characters.

Questions on language

- You may be asked to focus on the language.
  For example:

  How does Caliban's language show that he is fearful …?

  How do the characters use language to battle with each other …?

  How does Shakespeare build up a mood of tension …?

- You need to explain what the language shows, and **what effect** it has.

Top Tip!

Annotate a copy of the extract to show:
- what the language is actually saying
- the effect of language features.

What the language shows

- Think about what the language is actually saying. Each sentence will have a **purpose**, which could include:
  - to persuade
  - to flatter
  - to deceive
  - to hurt
  - to fill in the background for the audience.

- When commenting on a sentence, **explain** what its purpose is, e.g.
  - *Capulet shows that he is over-confident about how well he knows Juliet when he says 'I think she will be ruled in all respects by me.'*
  - *Ariel asks, 'Was't well done?' because he is trying to gain Prospero's favour so that he can be freed.*

What effect the language has

- You also need to comment on **how well** the language performs its purpose. Focus on Shakespeare's **expressive language**:

  Pages 78–9.

  - **imagery**, e.g. *Romeo's comparison of Juliet with 'a snowy dove trooping with crows' is appropriate because he sees her as pure and far more beautiful than other girls.*

  - **powerful words**, e.g. *Mercutio shows his disgust with Romeo's refusal to fight Tybalt by piling up adjectives: 'O calm, dishonourable, vile submission!'*

  - **sound effects**, e.g. *Caliban almost spits his curse on Prospero (note the repeated 's' sounds): 'all the infections that the sun sucks up'.*

  - **word play**, e.g. *Romeo and Mercutio show their friendship through playful sparring: When Mercutio says that 'dreamers often lie,' Romeo counters with 'In bed asleep, while they do dream things true'.*

This is the start of a level 7 answer to the question:

Comment on the purpose and effect of these lines from Act 4
Scene 3 of *Romeo and Juliet*.

Alack, alack, is it not like that I,
So early waking, what with loathsome smells,
And shrieks like mandrakes' torn out of the earth,
That living mortals, hearing them, run mad:–
O, if I wake, shall I not be distraught,
Environed with all these hideous fears?
And madly play with my forefather's joints?
And pluck the mangled Tybalt from his shroud?
And, in this rage, with some great kinsman's bone,
As with a club, dash out my desperate brains?

Did You Know?

Some of Shakespeare's plays are written completely in verse, such as *King John*, *Richard II* and *Henry VI Part 1*.

level
7

In this speech Juliet reveals her fears about taking the sleeping potion given to her by Friar Laurence. She does this vividly, asking herself questions that build to the climax of her taking her own life. The questions shows her uncertainty, while her unfinished sentence ('... run mad –') indicates that her intense anxiety prevents her from following a complete train of thought.

> the **purpose** of the language

> effective use of **quotation** throughout

These lines effectively show Juliet's fears about waking alone surrounded by dead bodies. They build up an intense picture of her fears – the 'loathsome smells', the 'shrieks like mandrakes', and how they might overwhelm her, making her so 'distraught' that she madly dashes out her 'desperate brains' with a bone. The word 'loathsome' is powerful and the comparison with mandrakes (supposed to shriek when uprooted) suggests something sinister. These ideas are especially vivid because they appeal to the senses of smell and hearing. The idea that she should 'madly play', like a child, with her 'forefather's joints', is shocking.

> the **effect** of the language – commenting on what makes it powerful

The repetition of 'Alack, alack' shows Juliet's distress and sense of helplessness. This is reinforced by the hard 'k' sounds in 'waking', 'shrieks' and 'mandrakes', suggesting the harshness of her situation. The near repetition of 'waking' and 'wake' emphasises her anxiety about the moment of waking.

> the **effect** of the language – commenting on how its sound reflects its meaning

Answering questions on performance

In the director's chair

The question may ask you to **imagine that you are directing** the set scenes, e.g.

> What advice would you give to the actor playing Prospero?

> How would you direct the scene to bring out the feeling between Romeo and Juliet?

> How would you build up tension in these scenes?

- As a director, you need to think about these aspects of the performance:
  - most importantly, the **acting** – how the actors say their lines, move about the stage and relate to other characters
  - the **set** and **costume design**, **lighting** and **sound**.

Answering the question

As you are the director, the ideas are up to you. However:

- You must **explain** why you are directing in a particular way. That means understanding what the characters are doing and why, e.g.
  He should sink to the ground at this point. ✗
  He is in complete despair, so he should sink to the ground at this point. ✓

- You must **link your ideas with the text** by quoting, e.g.
  When Romeo says 'I do protest, I never injured thee' he should make an open-handed gesture towards Tybalt to show that he bears him no ill will.

> **Top Tip!**
>
> Remember that Shakespeare wrote his plays to be performed, not to be read. Imagine the actors on stage as they say their lines – how could they best bring out the meaning of their words?

Focus on character, mood and development

- Bring out the **feelings** or **key features** of the character in your direction, e.g. *To show that his <u>anger</u> with Juliet makes him want to hit her, Capulet should raise his hand threateningly on his words 'My fingers itch'.*

- **Emphasise** a particular **mood** by varying the voice, or pace, or adding pauses, e.g. *Balthasar should <u>pause</u> after 'Then ...', and then <u>sound almost pleading</u> on '... she is well, and nothing can be ill'.*

- Show that a character or mood can **develop** or **change** through a scene, e.g. *Only when Ferdinand kneels before his father can Alonso believe that it is really him. His voice should show this by ...*

Here is part of a level 7 answer to the question:

How would you direct Caliban in *The Tempest* Act 1
Scene 2 to bring out his relationship with Prospero?

> Caliban should run onto the stage, hurling his
> curse at Prospero. Even after Prospero's response,
> which promises punishment, he should be defiant
> when he says 'This island's mine'. He should point
> accusingly at Prospero at 'Which thou takest
> from me'. This will underline how angry he feels
> with Prospero at losing his independence.

saying how Caliban should move

saying how Caliban should speak

point – evidence – comment, explaining the direction

Prospero and Caliban threaten and curse each other vehemently (Act 1 Scene 2, *The Tempest*).

Did You Know?

Shakespeare knew how to write for actors because he was an actor as well as a playwright.

Spot Check

True or false?
1 Shakespeare's plays were written to be read on the page.
2 When you are asked to be a director, you have to put on a performance.
3 You don't have to describe how the scenes would have been performed in Shakespeare's day.
4 You can include thoughts on the best lighting and sound.
5 You don't have to quote from the extracts in this kind of question.

To raise your level from level 6 to level 7, follow these guidelines.

Show your understanding

- Really think about how the **characters' speech and actions** relate to the main idea that you have to discuss. For example, if the question is about your impressions of Caliban, then think hard about how Caliban comes across in **every detail**.

- Focus on the **effect of Shakespeare's language**. Explain in detail how individual words and phrases show things about the character's feelings or thoughts, or about the wider ideas in the play, e.g. *The phrase 'great master' shows how much Ariel is a slave to Prospero.*

- Cover all the **main ideas** that you can think of, across **both extracts**.

- Don't be afraid of including **your own opinion**, as long as you can back it up.

- **Focus on the extracts** given, but try to show through your comments that you understand how they fit into the **play as a whole**, e.g. *As we see later in the play …*

Structure your answer

- **Plan** your answer, so that it is well organised and clear.

- Begin with a short **introduction** that sets the scene and refers to the key words in the question.

- End with a **conclusion** that sums up your answer to the question.

- Use **paragraphs** and **connectives** to show how your ideas are organised and linked, e.g. *When we come to Act 3, however, …*

- **Quote** from the extracts frequently, but only **to back up your points**. Short, embedded quotations are better than long quotations. Give a **comment** explaining why the quotation makes your point.

Top Tip!

Only tell the story of the scene (the plot) if it is relevant to the point you are making.

Look at the beginning of this level 7 answer to the question:

What impression do we get of Friar Laurence in Act 2 Scene 3 and Act 4 Scene 2?

level
7

Both scenes give the impression that Friar Laurence is a wise, sympathetic and fatherly man. In the second, however, he also shows himself ready to take a desperate action.

In the first scene Friar Laurence is presented as a philosophical man who appreciates nature, especially the 'powerful grace' of herbs. But he is wise and knows that 'Virtue itself turns vice, being misapplied', which makes him a good advisor to Romeo. He speaks in a friendly way when he says, 'Our Romeo hath not been in bed tonight', calls Romeo 'good son' when he says he has forgotten Rosaline, but 'chides' him for so quickly falling for Juliet.

Friar Laurence often delivers wise comments with the balanced neatness of proverbs: '... where care lodges, sleep will never lie.' He knows that for Romeo to be awake at dawn he must be troubled. Believing in straight talking, he tells Romeo, kindly but sternly, 'Riddling confession finds but riddling shrift.'

We see another side to Frair Laurence when he is prepared to give Juliet a desperate remedy: '... if thou darest, I'll give thee remedy'. He is also quite scheming:

Hold, then; go home, be merry, give consent
To marry Paris ...

He is deceiving Juliet's parents.

Good introduction – covers both extracts and refers to key words in question.

Good paragraph organisation – new point for each paragraph.

Tight focus throughout on impressions of Friar Laurence.

Notes the tone of the language.

Quotations are brief but relevant, and skilfully included in the sentences.

Shows an understanding of how different character aspects appear in each scene.

Did You Know?

William Shakespeare had eleven different ways of spelling his name.

Answers to Spot Check questions

p. 7 **1** d **2** c **3** a **4** b

p. 8 **1** plot, setting, language and characters **2** when things are sorted out at the end

p. 13 **1** to sell something; through powerful design, emotive words, clever slogans **2** that an opposing point is being made **3** to draw the reader in

p. 15 **1 a** opinion, **b** fact **2** 'Frankenstein foods' refers to the mad scientist who abused nature in his experiments, 'Food to feed our future' makes you think humans need GM foods for their future well-being, or even for the future of the species

p. 17 **1** biography = an account of someone else's life, autobiography = account of your own life **2** 1st person **3** true

p. 18 **1 a** personification, **b** metaphor, **c** simile **2 a** it makes the sun seem like the person not wanting to get up, **b** it draws a picture of the girl's (red) hair having the power and colour of flames, **c** it makes the writing seem aggressive, as the pen is described as a weapon

p. 21 **1** instruction **2** a direct command **3** in formal, impersonal writing, e.g. The house was built in 1897.

p. 22 **1** they show how the ideas are linked **2** information leaflet, history essay **3** (e.g.) by answering the question posed at the beginning

p. 25 **1** no **2** when you are introducing the other side (or the opponents) of the issue **3** to see whether you'd like to buy it; also to be entertained by the writing **4** a film

p. 27 **1** *It is important … is very formal, Can you up your water intake … is more friendly* **2** *That's wicked, man; It's really nice; It is perfectly delightful.*

p. 28 **1** true **2** false **3** false **4** false

p. 30 **1** suggest rather than state directly **2** understanding what the author is suggesting **3** true

p. 32 **1** (e.g.) to organise the passage into different points **2** (e.g.) information texts, advice leaflets, to break up the text and make it easy to see what each bit is for **3** (e.g.) it sets the tone straight away

p. 41 **1** false **2** true **3** false **4** true

p. 43 **1 a** argue, **b** instruct, **c** inform/describe, **d** persuade **2** keeping the point of view, formality and tone the same

p. 44 **1** false **2** true **3** true **4** false

p. 46 **1** (e.g.) atrocious, awful, terrible, useless, pathetic, dreadful **2** (e.g.) useless, pathetic, awful, dreadful, terrible, atrocious **3** fab

p. 49 **1** (e.g.) Kevin took the bus to town. He didn't want to miss the start of the film, so he pushed through the crowds. **2** Kevin took the bus to town. Not wanting to miss the start of the film, he pushed through the crowds. **3** Midge was given a hard time by his mother.

p. 51 **1** (e.g.) when there is a new time, a new place or a new character **2** false **3** (e.g.) a clear introduction, an exciting piece of action that makes you want to read on **4** a sentence that gives the main point of the paragraph

p. 53 letter: 1, 3, 5, speech: 2, 4, 6

p. 55 **1** to begin sentences, to begin proper names **2** Graeme's mobile rang. It was Paula calling from Oxford. **3** 'It's endless, isn't it?' she said, looking at the minutes go by. **4** a colon leads the reader forward, whereas a semi-colon is used for two balanced clauses.

p. 57 **1** He used the colours red, white and blue, to which he added yellow as an afterthought. **2** Lucy, the youngest of the children, is really the most important character. **3** Because he played so badly, Stuart was replaced at half-time.

p. 59 **1** flys (flies), gasses (gases) **2** skating – skated, skidding – skidded, respecting – respected, benefiting – benefited **3** dived, stole, travelled, bought **4** (e.g.) disbelieve, unbelievable.

p. 60 **1** quitely (quietly), dissappoint (disappoint), beleive (believe), neccessary (necessary) **2** 'accept' means take, 'except' means apart from

p. 63 **1** a narrative written using s/he **2** false **3** a cliffhanger is a deliberate ending chosen to keep readers guessing, whereas an unfinished ending is unplanned **4** (e.g.) keep speech short, begin a new paragraph for each speaker, mix speech and action

p. 65 **1** (e.g.) they help you brainstorm ideas and order the ideas **2** no **3** they are describing words **4** a way of comparing something directly with something else by saying it is that thing

p. 67 **1** false **2** because the explanation itself should be written one step at a time **3** causal connectives, e.g. because, when, therefore **4** the main facts are given in the first one or two paragraphs; a snappy headline

p. 69 **1** discussion **2** (e.g.) write one paragraph presenting the views 'for', then one presenting the views 'against' an issue **3** false **4** (e.g.) however, on the other hand, in addition

p. 71 **1** you give each point of your argument a new paragraph **2** (e.g.) repetition, emotive words, rhetorical questions **3** good **4** advice

p. 75 **1** true **2** false **3** true **4** true

p. 77 **1** (e.g.) because people thought a lot about what it meant to be a king **2** (e.g.) theatre was more popular then, and plays were performed during the day (in the light) **3** (e.g.) there is a happy ending, there are misunderstandings

p. 79 **1** unrhymed verse **2** for the lower class characters **3** when words begin with similar sounds **4** simile (guilt compared to poison) and personification (guilt 'bites')

p. 81 **1** b **2** d **3** a **4** c

p. 83 **1** refer to key words in the question and refer to the context **2** to show that you are basing your ideas on the play and that you understand the play **3** how to use evidence from the extracts: make your own point, then quote from the extract to back it up, then explain how the quote does this **4** for comparison, to show that you are drawing similarities between your ideas.

p. 90 **1** false **2** false **3** true **4** true **5** false

Glossary

adjective a describing word, e.g. 'red', 'evil'

advice a text type which has the aim of suggesting a course of action

alliteration the effect created when words next to each other begin with the same letter (e.g. 'terrible twins')

analyse to investigate something carefully and thoroughly

apostrophe a punctuation mark used to show either possession (e.g. 'Dave's computer') or a missing letter (e.g. 'can't')

argument a text that presents and develops a particular point of view

audience someone who listens to or reads a text

bias weighting a text unfairly in favour of one side or the other

blank verse in Shakespeare's plays, unrhymed verse with 10 syllables in each line

characterisation how an author presents and develops their characters

clause a group of words in a sentence which expresses a single idea; a clause has a verb and usually a subject

colon a punctuation mark that introduces a clause that leads on from or explains another clause

comedy a Shakespearean play about relationships with a happy ending

command a verb that gives an instruction to the reader, e.g. 'Think about your children …'

complex sentence a sentence with one main clause and one or more subordinate clauses

compound sentence a sentence made up of two or more simple sentences linked by 'and', 'but' or 'or'

connective a word or phrase which links clauses and sentences, to signal to the audience where the text is going

direct address using the second person ('you') to hold the reader's attention in a text

discussion a text type which helps the audience understand an issue by presenting the different viewpoints fairly

emotive language words, phrases and ideas designed to make the audience feel something strongly

explanation a text type which helps the audience understand why or how something is as it is

fact a piece of knowledge or information that can be proved to be true

fiction anything that is made up, especially a story

formal language writing or speech that follows the strictest rules of Standard English

homophone a word that sounds the same as another but is spelt differently, e.g. 'where' and 'wear'

imagery the use of language to create an image or picture; *see also* simile, metaphor, personification

informal language language that does not follow the strict rules of Standard English

information a text type which presents facts in a way that is easy to understand

instruction a text type which tells the audience how to do something, through a series of sequenced steps

inverted comma a punctuation mark used to show the beginning and end of direct speech

media the term given to texts aimed at large numbers of people, e.g. television, magazines, newspapers, Internet

metaphor a type of imagery which describes something as something else, e.g. 'you are an island'

motivation why a character behaves as he or she does

non-fiction any text that is not made up

opinion a person's own view about something

paragraph a group of sentences on one topic, person or event. A new paragraph begins a new line.

paraphrase to summarise part of the text in your own words

person a way of referring to pronouns and verbs according to whether they indicate the speaker/writer (1st person: 'I', 'we'), the audience (2nd person: 'you') or someone else (3rd person: 's/he', 'it', 'they')

personification a type of imagery which refers to objects as if they were human, e.g. 'the sun punished them'

persuasion a text type which has the aim of selling an idea or a product

phrase a group of words which go together, e.g. 'the garden gate'

plot the storyline

popular newspaper a newspaper that aims to entertain as much as to inform its readers, e.g. *The Sun, The Mirror*

prefix letters added at the start of a word to change its meaning

punctuation a way of marking text with symbols to make the meaning clear

purpose the aim of a text

recount a text type which tells the reader what happened, often in an informative and entertaining way

relative clause part of the sentence beginning 'who', 'which', 'that' etc. which gives more information about the main clause

rhetorical question a question asked for effect, not for an answer

rhetorical technique a technique used to persuade an audience, e.g. emotive language, sound effects, repetition, rhetorical questions

romance a Shakespearean play that mixes elements of tragedy and comedy

scan to look over a text quickly in order to find a particular word or piece of information

semi-colon a punctuation mark used to show a pause in a sentence longer than a comma

simile a type of imagery which compares something with something else, making the comparison clear by using a phrase such as 'like; or 'as if', e.g. 'she swam like a fish'

simple sentence a sentences with only one clause

skim to read a whole text quickly

slogan a memorable phrase used to sell a product

Standard English the type of spoken and written English that is generally considered 'correct' and that is taught in schools

suffix letters added at the end of a word to change its meaning

summarise to identify the key points of a text

text a block of spoken or written language

theme the underlying ideas or issues that a story or play deals with

tone a measure of the quality, mood or style of a piece of writing

topic sentence the main sentence in a paragraph, which gives the topic (subject) of the paragraph

tragedy a Shakespearean play with an unhappy ending

verb a word that refers to an action, e.g. 'runs' or a state of being, e.g. 'feels'

Index

Collins Revision

KS3 English Workbook

Lucy English

Reading skills

When we think of reading we tend to just think of being able to understand the words and the story. However, there's more to being a great reader than that!

Being a great reader means you are able to pick out specific words and phrases from the text to act as evidence for your ideas. You are also able to look beyond surface meaning and make **deductions** and **interpret information**. Great readers can also work out and explain how a text works – this means looking at the **structure** and **organisation** such as the layout or how the writing develops. The language of the text is something students often find difficult to write about, but a great reader is able to do just that and explain how a word or phrase creates a particular meaning. Finally, great readers are able to identify and comment on why a text has been written and what the author intended it to do.

All of these features of a great reader have been broken down into different Assessment Focuses for KS3 and you will encounter them during your English lessons and in your Teacher Assessment at the end of Year 9.

Reading Assessment Focuses

AF1: use a range of strategies, including accurate decoding of text, to read for meaning.

This means you are able to read beyond the surface meaning of the text and can work out any connotations and implications.

AF2: understand, describe, select or retrieve information, events or ideas from texts and use quotation and reference to text

This means you need to show you understand what you have read by picking ideas and evidence out of the text. You can also put events and ideas in your own words.

AF3: deduce, infer or interpret information, events or ideas from texts

This means you can make links between ideas. You read between the lines and work out the story or idea that is implied.

AF4: identify and comment on the structure and organisation of texts, including grammatical and presentational features at text level

This means you can explain how and why the text is structured in the way it is. This might refer to layout or how the writing develops.

AF5: explain and comment on writers' use of language, including grammatical and literary features at word and sentence level

This means you can write about the language of the text and explain why certain words or phrases have been used and the effect they have on the reader.

AF6: identify and comment on writers' purposes and viewpoints and the overall effect of the text on the reader

This means you can look at the big picture – you can explain why the writer has written the text and what they were trying to do. You can also explain what impact the whole text has on the reader.

The texts

This part of your KS3 English pack contains ten practice reading texts for you to work through. Each text has a series of questions that test your reading skills. These questions all test a different Assessment Focus, just as in your English lessons and in your final Teacher Assessment.

It doesn't matter how long you spend on these tasks – in fact, it's better to take the time you need to make sure your answers are brilliant! To check your answers, turn to the back of the book.

The first thing you will need to do when you read each text is to work out the **purpose**, **audience** and **text type**. This will help you with the questions that follow. It's really good to get into the habit of using this skill whenever you are reading or writing as it will help ensure you are great at both.

Good luck!

1

Read the extract and answer the questions that follow.

This is the opening of a book called *Raven's Gate*, by Anthony Horowitz.

Matt Freeman knew he was making a mistake.

He was sitting on a low wall outside Ipswich station, wearing a grey hooded sweatshirt, shapeless, faded jeans, and trainers with frayed laces. It was six o'clock in the evening and the London train had just pulled in. Behind him, commuters were fighting their way out of the station. The concourse was a tangle of cars, taxis and pedestrians, all of them trying to find their way home. A traffic light blinked from red to green but nothing moved. Somebody leant on their horn and the noise blared out, cutting through the damp evening air. Matt heard it and looked up briefly. But the crowd meant nothing to him. He wasn't part of it. He never had been – and he sometimes thought he never would be.

- Purpose = _____

- Audience = _____

- Text type = _____

1 Matt is made to seem an outsider. Find one quotation that shows he does not fit in.

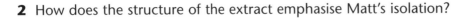

_____

_____

1 mark

2 How does the structure of the extract emphasise Matt's isolation?

_____

_____

_____

_____

2 marks

3 The table below gives examples of descriptive language used in the text.
Complete the table to explain the impression each word or phrase gives.

Example of descriptive language	The impression it gives
'commuters were fighting their way out of the station'	This gives the impression of pressure and chaos.
'a tangle of cars, taxis and pedestrians'	
'Somebody leant on their horn and the noise blared out'	

2 marks

4 The extract emphasises Matt's feeling of isolation and not belonging.
Explain how the whole extract creates this impression.
Support your ideas with quotations from the extract.

_____

_____

_____

_____

_____

_____

_____

_____

_____

3 marks

5 What sort of thing do you think might happen next? Provide evidence for
your answer.

_____

_____

_____

_____

_____

_____

_____

2 marks

2

Read the extract and answer the questions that follow.

> This is from a book called *The Boy in the Striped Pyjamas*, by John Boyne. It is about a nine-year-old boy called Bruno.
>
> Bruno narrowed his eyes and wished he were taller, stronger and eight years older. A ball of anger exploded inside him and made him wish that he had the courage to say exactly what he wanted to say. It was one thing, he decided, to be told what to do by Mother and Father – that was perfectly reasonable and to be expected – but it was another thing entirely to be told what to do by someone else. Even by someone with a fancy title like 'Lieutenant'.

Getting to grips with the text

- Purpose = _____
- Audience = _____
- Text type = _____

1 Why is Bruno angry?

_____

1 mark

2 The writer describes the way Bruno is feeling very clearly. Identify two words or phrases that show his anger.

_____

_____

1 mark

3 Complete the table, explaining what each of these quotations tells us about Bruno's state of mind.

Quotation	What it tells us about Bruno's state of mind
'Bruno narrowed his eyes and wished he were taller, stronger and eight years older'	
'A ball of anger exploded inside him'	

2 marks

4 What is Bruno's attitude towards the Lieutenant? Provide a quotation to support your answer.

_____

_____

_____

5 Bruno refers to his parents as 'Mother' and 'Father'. Why does this make him seem young?

_____

_____

_____

_____

6 The writer makes us take Bruno's side in this extract. How has he done this?

_____

_____

_____

_____

_____

_____

_____

_____

_____

_____

_____

_____

_____

_____

_____

_____

_____

_____

_____

_____

3

Read the extract and answer the questions that follow.

Young people can take centre stage this summer with Woking Borough Council's arts workshops.

Calling all budding actors and artists! There is a packed programme of activities lined up this summer to get your creative juices really flowing.

If you fancy yourself as an actor, why not join one of the **drama workshops** at the Rhonda McGaw theatre? These will give you a chance to develop your theatre skills while exploring some exciting scripts from top writers including Salman Rushdie and Timberlake Wertenbaker.

You'll have lots of fun learning new skills and meeting other young people with a flair for the stage. And you can show off your talents when you invite family and friends to a final performance at the end of the week.

Or if you'd like to see behind the screen at the Rhoda McGaw theatre, you can sign up for a **cinema crafts workshop** in August. You'll be able to make your own costumes and props for the show for the afternoon film. The workshops are suitable for children aged 7–11, and discounts for Passport to Leisure holders are available.

Crafty types aged between 7 and 11 can make their mark at **arts workshops** at Woking Youth Arts Centre, Knaphill, on 27th or 28th July. Try African drumming or make your own Mexican crafts at a Holiday Fiesta workshop – and take your creations home at the end of the day.

The Craft Co. will also be running workshops for children aged 6 and above at The Barn in Worplesdon throughout August. There's a huge range of activities available, including T-shirt painting, salt-dough modelling, card-making and pot-decorating.

Young dancers and poets aged between 8 and 16 have their chance to shine between 22nd and 26th August at Woking College Dance Studio.

Working with professional dancers, you can contribute your ideas to a new words and movement experience. Friends and family are welcome to watch the final performance on Friday afternoon.

- Purpose = _____

- Audience = _____

- Text type = _____

Getting to grips with the text

1 This article outlines summer activities for young people in Woking. Give one activity that will be available and some details of what it will include.

_____

_____

2 The language used makes the opportunities sound exciting.
Complete the table to explain what the language suggests in each example.

Example of language used	What it suggests
'a packed programme'	The alliteration makes it sound fun and exciting.
'a huge range of activities'	
'chance to shine'	

3 How does the whole article make the opportunities available for young people in Woking during the summer seem exciting and attractive?
You should comment on how the extract:
• Makes the activities seem exciting and fun
• Makes it seem easy to join, even if you don't know anyone
• Uses presentation and layout devices to help the reader find the information they might be interested in.

_____

_____

_____

_____

_____

_____

_____

_____

_____

_____

_____

_____

_____

_____

_____

_____

4

Read the letter and answer the questions that follow.

LeisureTime Plus
Rock Hill Road
Sheffield
01234 567890

Dear Ms Holroyd,

Everybody knows the need to live a healthy lifestyle but did you know that regular exercise can boost your immune system and improve your energy levels by up to 50%? Experts have shown that people who exercise for just 30 minutes three times a week are fitter, healthier and happier. At LeisureTime Plus we want to help you reach this state.

Forget all you might think about crowded, sweaty gyms and sergeant-major fitness instructors with the bark of a bulldog; our staff and facilities are second to none and help to make exercise fun and rewarding. We're not saying it's going to be a walk in the park, but we'll be with you all the way as you travel your journey to a fitter, happier you.

Just think, in four weeks you'll notice your skin will have a new, radiant glow, in six weeks your jeans will be easier to do up, and in twelve weeks you'll be running up flights of stairs without a thought. Sound good? Well just sign up for our fabulous new introductory offer today and this could be your reality.

Call LeisureTime Plus today for more details, we're looking forward to helping find the new you.

Yours truly,

Malcolm Day

Director, LeisureTime Plus

- Purpose = _____

- Audience = _____

- Text type = _____

Getting to grips with the text

1 What does this letter want the reader to do?

_____

1 mark

2 The letter is addressed to a specific person, Ms Holroyd. What sort of person does the letter suggest Ms Holroyd is?

_____

_____

2 marks

3 Explain two different ways in which the letter makes exercise sound appealing.

- _____
- _____

4 The letter uses negative phrases to describe bad fitness experiences.
Fill in the table to explain why the language is used in this way.

Example of negative phrase	Why the language is used in this way
'crowded, sweaty gyms'	
'sergeant-major fitness instructors with the bark of a bulldog'	

5 The letter uses informal, colloquial phrases. Identify one of these phrases and explain why it is used.

- Informal, colloquial phrase: _____
- Why it is used: _____

6 Explain how this letter makes joining LeisureTime Plus seem a good idea.
In your answer you should write about:
- The use of fact and opinion
- The tone of the letter
- The use of language.

_____
_____
_____
_____
_____
_____
_____
_____
_____
_____
_____
_____
_____
_____

5

Read the newspaper article and answer the questions that follow.

SCHOOLKIDS TO BE GIVEN MOBILE PHONES

Government heralds a huge step forward in learning technology

Government ministers were celebrating yesterday after announcing a deal with mobile phone manufacturers to give these gadgets to all schoolchildren. They are confident the newest range of phones will help students learn in today's techno-world.

Wayne Daniels, advisor for education, said this move would enable children to interact with lessons in a modern way as they could be used as personal organisers and even record parts of lessons. "Students won't be able to claim they forgot to do their homework," he said, "not when it's recorded onto the phone's organiser with an alarm set for that evening."

Backers of this scheme reel off lists of benefits: students will be able to use the organiser, the memo facility, research using the Internet, share ideas in class, manipulate sounds in music; there's even the alarm to get them up in the morning and prevent them being late for school!

However, teachers are questioning this move, claiming that phones are a nuisance, constantly interrupting lessons and providing a target for bullies and thieves. They demand to know how much money has been spent on this project, and suggest some of this could have been spent improving the many dilapidated school buildings around the country.

Students, meanwhile, were celebrating!

Getting to grips with the text

- Purpose = _____
- Audience = _____
- Text type = _____

1 Identify two ways that it is claimed mobile phones will help students' learning.

- _____
- _____

1 mark

2 How does the writer show that the teachers' views are going to be different from the views already described in the article?

_____

3 What does the phrase 'today's techno-world' suggest?

_____

_____

4 What is the effect of having a quotation from the education advisor?

_____

_____

5 Some of the language used in the paragraph about the teachers' response is very negative. Pick two negative words or phrases and explain the impression they create.

- _____

_____

_____

- _____

_____

_____

6 Does this article present all views in a balanced way? Use evidence to support your ideas.

_____

_____

_____

_____

_____

_____

_____

_____

_____

_____

_____

_____

_____

6

Read the poem and answer the questions that follow.

> **Blackberry Picking**
> (for Philip Hobsbaum)
> *by Seamus Heaney*
>
> Late August, given heavy rain and sun
> For a full week, the blackberries would ripen.
> At first, just one, a glossy purple clot
> Among others, red, green, hard as a knot.
> You ate that first one and its flesh was sweet
> Like thickened wine: summer's blood was in it
> Leaving stains upon the tongue and lust for
> Picking. Then red ones inked up and that hunger
> Sent us out with milk-cans, pea-tins, jam-pots
> Where briars scratched and wet grass bleached our boots.
> Round hayfields, cornfields and potato-drills
> We trekked and picked until the cans were full,
> Until the tinkling bottom had been covered
> With green ones, and on top big blobs burned
> Like a plate of eyes. Our hands were peppered
> With thorn pricks, our palms sticky as Bluebeard's.
>
> We hoarded the fresh berries in the byre.
> But when the bath was filled we found a fur,
> A rat-grey fungus, glutting on our cache.
> The juice was stinking too. Once off the bush
> The fruit fermented, the sweet flesh would turn sour.
> I always felt like crying. It wasn't fair
> That all the lovely canfuls smelt of rot.
> Each year I hoped they'd keep, knew they would not.

Bluebeard was a savage murderer who killed his first six wives.
briars = the long, thorny stems that blackberries grow on
cache = a collection, store or treasure

• Purpose = _____	**Getting to grips with the text**
• Audience = _____	
• Text type = _____	

1 The poem describes blackberry picking. Every year the narrator tries to pick and keep blackberries but isn't able to. What happens?

_____

1 mark

2 The narrator says they collected the blackberries in 'milk-cans, pea-tins, jam-pots'. What does this suggest about the blackberry collectors?

_____

1 mark

3 What is the impact of the final line?

_____

1 mark

4 Find and write down an example of a simile. Explain why the poet has used this image.

Simile: _____

1 mark

Explanation: _____

_____

_____

2 marks

5 The blackberry pickers work hard to collect their fruit. What impression do you get of them? Use quotations as evidence for your ideas.

_____

_____

_____

_____

_____

_____

_____

5 marks

_____

6 The poet wrote this poem as an adult, looking back on a childhood memory. What impression does he give us of this memory?

_____

_____

_____

_____

_____

_____

_____

_____

_____

5 marks

_____

Read the extract and answer the questions that follow.

How to make the scrummiest pizza

You will need:
- Plain pizza bases – you can make these using the recipe on page 12 or buy them from the supermarket
- Tomato topping – see page 14 for our tasty topping
- Mozzarella – sliced
- Your fave toppings – slice these up and put them in bowls ready to use.

These are our fave toppings:
- Ham, mushroom and sweetcorn
- Pepperoni, green peppers, mushrooms and more pepperoni
- BBQ chicken (you can get this ready cooked from the supermarket), ham and pepper
- Cheese and tomato (sometimes simple is best!)
- Prawns and spinach (honestly!)
- Peppers, mushrooms and pineapple

How to do it:

1 First, take your pizza base and plaster it with the tomato topping. Don't let this go over the edge as it'll slide off and burn in the oven!

2 Next place slices of mozzarella on the tomato – it's up to you how much you like.

3 Now for the fun bit: carefully position your favourite toppings on your pizza. There are no rules but we've found it's best to have between 2 and 5 different toppings.

4 When you are happy with your creation, carefully put it in a hot oven (180–200°C) for 12–20 minutes, depending on the size of the pizza and the amount of topping you have. It's probably best to set the timer to check it after 10 minutes. It's also a good idea to ask an adult to help with this bit.

5 You'll know when it's ready to enjoy because the cheese will have melted and it'll look and smell mouth-watering! Take it out of the oven carefully (get someone to help with this), put it on a plate and enjoy!

Don't forget the boring washing-up bit – it's worth it if you want to use the kitchen again!

- Purpose = _____
- Audience = _____
- Text type = _____

Getting to grips with the text

1 Put numbers in the boxes to show the correct order to do these things:

Put the mozzarella on the pizza	☐	Put your favourite toppings on the pizza	☐
Make the tomato topping	☐	Put the pizza in the oven	☐

1 mark

2 Who is the intended audience of this text? Explain how you know.

_____

_____

_____

3 The language of this text helps to make it clear and easy to follow. Choose a word or phrase that is used to make it easy to follow and explain how it does this.

_____

_____

_____

4 This text uses informal language and phrases. Identify an informal word or phrase and explain why it has been used.

_____

_____

_____

5 In the list of 'our fave toppings' there are comments in brackets. Explain why it says '(sometimes simple is best!)' after 'Cheese and tomato'.

_____

_____

6 Do you think this text is likely to make young people want to make the pizza? You should comment on how the text:
- Makes the recipe seem fun
- Makes a connection with the reader
- Makes the recipe seem easy.

_____

_____

_____

_____

_____

_____

_____

_____

_____

_____

_____

8

Read the extract from *An Arrest*, by Ambrose Bierce, and answer the questions that follow on pages 116–117.

Having murdered his brother-in-law, Orrin Brower of Kentucky was a fugitive from justice. From the county jail where he had been confined to await his trial he had escaped by knocking down his jailer with an iron bar, robbing him of his keys and, opening the outer door, walking out into the night. The jailer being unarmed, Brower got no weapon with which to defend his recovered liberty. As soon as he was out of the town he had the folly to enter a forest; this was many years ago, when that region was wilder than it is now.

The night was pretty dark, with neither moon nor stars visible, and as Brower had never dwelt thereabout, and knew nothing of the lay of the land, he was, naturally, not long in losing himself. He could not have said if he were getting farther away from the town or going back to it – a most important matter to Orrin Brower. He knew that in either case a posse of citizens with a pack of bloodhounds would soon be on his track and his chance of escape was very slender; but he did not wish to assist in his own pursuit. Even an added hour of freedom was worth having.

Suddenly he emerged from the forest into an old road, and there before him saw, indistinctly, the figure of a man, motionless in the gloom. It was too late to retreat: the fugitive felt that at the first movement back toward the wood he would be, as he afterward explained, "filled with buckshot". So the two stood there like trees, Brower nearly suffocated by the activity of his own heart; the other – the emotions of the other are not recorded.

A moment later – it may have been an hour – the moon sailed into a patch of unclouded sky and the hunted man saw that visible embodiment of Law lift an arm and point significantly toward and beyond him. He understood. Turning his back to his captor, he walked submissively away in the direction indicated, looking to neither the right nor the left; hardly daring to breathe, his head and back actually aching with a prophecy of buckshot.

Brower was as courageous a criminal as ever lived to be hanged; that was shown by the conditions of awful personal peril in which he had coolly killed his brother-in-law. It is needless to relate them here; they came out at his trial, and the revelation of his calmness

in confronting them came near to saving his neck. But what would you have? – when a brave man is beaten, he submits.

So they pursued their journey jailward along the old road through the woods. Only once did Brower venture a turn of the head: just once, when he was in deep shadow and he knew that the other was in moonlight, he looked backward. His captor was Burton Duff, the jailer, as white as death and bearing upon his brow the livid mark of the iron bar. Orrin Brower had no further curiosity.

Eventually they entered the town, which was all alight, but deserted; only the women and children remained, and they were off the streets. Straight toward the jail the criminal held his way. Straight up to the main entrance he walked, laid his hand upon the knob of the heavy iron door, pushed it open without command, entered and found himself in the presence of a half-dozen armed men. Then he turned. Nobody else entered.

On a table in the corridor lay the dead body of Burton Duff.

• Purpose = _____

• Audience = _____

• Text type = _____

Getting to grips with the text

1 Why is Orrin Brower a 'fugitive from justice'?

_____

_____

2 What is the name of the jailer?

_____

3 The table gives examples of descriptive words and phrases used in the text.
Fill in the table to explain the impression each word or phrase gives.

Example of descriptive phrase	Impression it creates
'the moon sailed into a patch of unclouded sky'	The moon is free and moves easily. This contrasts with the actions of the fugitive.
'as white as death'	
'the livid mark of the iron bar'	

4 The first sentence of the story gives us lots of background information.

   a Explain what it tells us.

   _____

   _____

   b Explain why it includes so much information in one sentence.

   _____

   _____

5 The story includes hints that the man who is making Orrin return to the jail is a ghost. Identify one of these hints and explain why it is used.

_____

_____

_____

_____

6 Look again at the last two paragraphs. How does the structure of the piece
make the ending dramatic?

_____

_____

_____

_____

_____

_____

_____

_____

_____

_____

_____

_____

_____

_____

_____

_____

_____

5 marks

9

Read the extract and answer the questions that follow.

 ★★★★★

Another cracking adventure with Wallace and Gromit

It's hard to believe it's been ten long years since Wallace last put the poor long-suffering Gromit through his paces, but now they're back, and with more gadgets than ever before! Yes, Wallace and Gromit hit the big screen, big time in a big full-length movie guaranteed to delight movie-goers of all ages.

From the moment the cheese-loving Wallace reappears on our screens, it's clear that Nick Park and his fellow animators haven't lost their touch, or their sense of humour. This film is not only a great story, but is also littered with jokes, from the 'Smug' fridge to the Austin Powers-type double entendres about melons.

The Plasticine models are a joy to see, full of fingerprints and energy in a way Computer Generated Imagery can never be. Furthermore, the voices are perfect for their characters; I even forgot superstars such as Helena Bonham-Carter and Ralph Fiennes were 'playing' Lady Tottington and Victor Quartermaine. Maybe that means they weren't really needed?

The plot isn't always as fast-moving as it could be, perhaps that's so they can make it the full-length film this is, but it's a hugely satisfying watch and justly deserving of its Oscar.

 Getting to grips with the text

- Purpose = _____

- Audience = _____

- Text type = _____

1 This extract was written to review the film and express the reviewer's opinion. Explain why the stars have been put at the top of the review.

_____

1 mark

2 The review uses lots of adjectives. Identify a phrase using adjectives and explain what effect their use has.

_____

_____

_____

 1 mark

3 What technique has the reviewer used here, and what impact does it have?

'Yes, Wallace and Gromit hit the big screen, big time in a big full-length movie guaranteed to delight movie-goers of all ages.'

_____

_____

_____

2 marks

4 This is a review, so it is giving the writer's opinion. However, it does contain some facts. Identify a fact and explain why it has been used.

_____

_____

_____

2 marks

5 The review uses a friendly and informal tone. Identify a word or phrase that is friendly and informal and explain why it has been used.

_____

_____

_____

2 marks

6 The review ends with 'it's a hugely satisfying watch and justly deserving of its Oscar'. Explain how the whole of the review supports this opinion.

_____

_____

_____

_____

_____

_____

_____

_____

_____

_____

_____

_____

_____

_____

_____

_____

5 marks

10

Read the extract and answer the questions that follow.

BORDONDOWN SCHOOL
LONGFIELD ROAD
BATH

Dear Parent

Thank you for your interest in our school. I am pleased to enclose a school prospectus and invitation to our next open day.

As you know Bordondown is a thriving school where staff and students work hard for top results. We are lucky to have some very talented members of the school community and we are looking forward to another year of excellent examination results, with many of our students going on to Oxbridge and other top universities.

The focus of every school day is learning, and every activity is geared to support your child in their journey to become a successful learner; perhaps he or she will be one of our Oxbridge students of the future?

Learning is the key to a successful life, and we insist on discipline in order to achieve it. From correct uniform to homework being completed on time, we find an organised student is a successful student.

In addition to the timetabled day, there are many extra-curricular activities available for your child; a browse through the booklet in the prospectus will outline some of these.

Although the prospectus provides a comprehensive guide to our school, the best way to find out about its workings is to visit us. We would be delighted to show you round the school, provide students for you to talk to, and answer any questions you might have. These tours do get very busy, so please book a place by returning the form or telephoning the office.

I look forward to meeting you soon,

Yours faithfully,

Matthew Best

Head teacher

Oxbridge: Oxford and Cambridge Universities

- Purpose = _____

- Audience = _____

- Text type = _____

> **Getting to grips with the text**

1 Why has the head teacher written this letter?

_____

2 Mr Best writes about the success some students have had:
'many of our students going on to Oxbridge and other top universities.'
What does this suggest he regards as school success?

_____

_____

_____

3 Although this letter is from one person, he uses the plural pronoun 'we'
throughout. Suggest why he does this and what impression he is trying
to give.

_____

_____

_____

4 The letter uses very short paragraphs. Explain why.

_____

_____

5 What impression of Bordondown School is created by this letter?

_____

_____

_____

_____

_____

_____

_____

_____

_____

_____

_____

_____

_____

Practice reading paper

Try this practice reading paper.

Make sure you are in a quiet place and can spend 1 hour 15 minutes without being disturbed.

You are allowed 15 minutes reading time in the test, so set a timer or ask someone to tell you when the reading time is up.

- Spend 15 minutes reading pages 123–129 and highlighting or marking the purpose, audience and text type of each text. You might also like to mark any interesting style or language features.

- When the 15 minutes reading time is up, you can turn to the question paper. You have 1 hour to answer the questions.

- There are 14 questions about these texts and they are worth 32 marks in total.

- Remember to look at the marks available and make sure you provide enough information to get full marks.

Blood

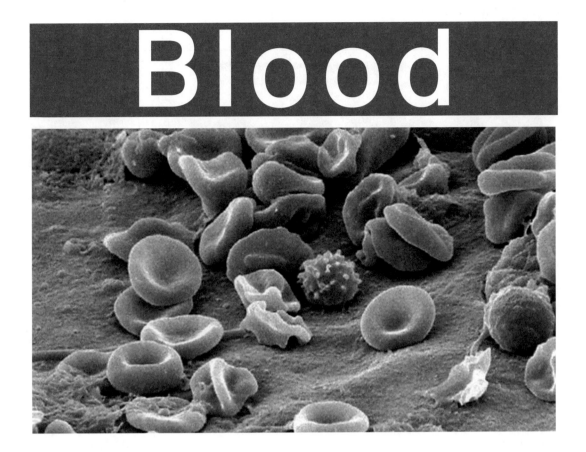

Contents

The texts in this booklet are all about blood. They explain the scientific facts about blood, and what it can tell us about people.

This is an extract from a booklet written for people who give blood. It gives information about the different colours blood can be and explains what this says about the donor.

Shades of red

What does the colour of your blood say about you?

Have you ever wondered why your blood seems to be a different shade of red from the donor on the next bed? Have you been concerned your blood looks more like Ribena than the finest Merlot? Although all blood is red, the shades vary between donors and can even be used to indicate health issues.

On average there are 35 trillion red blood cells, suspended in plasma, circulating in your body at any one time. Red cells are filled with haemoglobin that gives your blood its red colour.

Blood naturally changes colour during its journey around your body. When you take a breath, the inhaled oxygen in your lungs attaches itself to haemoglobin in the red cells. At this point your blood is oxygenated and a strong, bright poppy-red.

On their journey around your body, red cells exchange oxygen for carbon dioxide which returns to

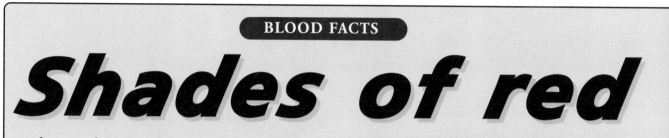

Our scientific staff have developed methods of visually checking the colour of your donation, as an additional safety measure. Much like a decorator's colour chart, donations are compared to a set of standard colour shades. Using colourmetric standards is another way we can help provide safer blood to the patient.

your lungs through your veins. The carbon dioxide is exhaled and the whole process begins again. At the end of the journey, your blood will appear a darker shade of red.

Blood is the transport system of your body. It not only carries energy to the cells but it also carries anything else that you ingest or absorb through your skin. Which also helps to explain why not everyone's blood is the same shade.

Having bright red blood is not necessarily a sign of good health. Heavy smokers may produce a vividly coloured donation because carbon monoxide in cigarette smoke is attached much more easily to red cells than oxygen. The blood is bright red because of the presence of a cherry-red compound called carboxyhaemoglobin, which forms when carbon monoxide binds to haemoglobin.

If blood looks pinkish, it may be due to a high level of water insoluble fats, called lipaemia. Lipaemia can be inherited or caused by a fatty diet.

Wine buffs may like to know that claret-coloured blood suggests haemoglobin may be leaking from the red cells; a natural part of blood's ageing process called haemolysis.

Colour match

You might be surprised to know our staff back at the centres look out for darker donations because deep shades imply possible bacterial contamination or incorrect storage. They are also vigilant for blood which appears to be clumped or

clotted or which looks darker in patches and may be unsuitable for transfusion.

The colour of plasma, which is usually straw-yellow, also varies enormously. Its colour can be seen after the blood has been separated, and the red cells removed. Some oral contraceptives turn plasma bright green and self-tanning pills may make it go a fluorescent orange!

Plasma is usually a clear yellow. However, it can look cloudy occasionally. This can be caused by a number of things. You could simply have eaten some fatty food before giving blood, or it could be caused by an underlying condition related to a high fat content in the body. It may even indicate a problem with the donation in relation to bacteria.

Our staff are trained to notice these differences and

act accordingly. In most cases colour and cloudiness are not a problem. But, in rare instances, it might mean referring the donor to their GP, or in the case of possible bacterial contamination, not using the donation, just to be on the safe side.

So, the next time you tuck into an oily curry the night before you donate, have a think about what colour your blood might be.

Did you know...

The importance of blood colour has endured through history, surviving in expressions we use today. The term 'blue-blooded', implying that someone is royal, was taken from the Spanish sangre azul and was adopted by the English in the 1830s. The English aristocracy spent little time outdoors in the sunlight and powdered and painted their skin white. Commoners believed that aristocrats had blue blood in their veins as this was how the veins appeared through such pale, translucent skin. Another well-known expression, 'red-blooded', now means 'vigorous' or 'virile' but may have originated from male warriors returning from battle and being bloodied.

Merlot and **claret** are both types of red wine.

This is an extract from a GCSE Science textbook. It explains about the chemical properties of blood.

A recipe for blood

On average a human adult has about five litres of blood inside them. About 40% of blood is made up of blood cells. There are three kinds of blood cell.

Red blood cells

There are 25 million million of these in an adult's body. They contain the red pigment haemoglobin and their main function is to carry oxygen from the lungs to the cells of the body. These cells live for about four months and are continually replaced.

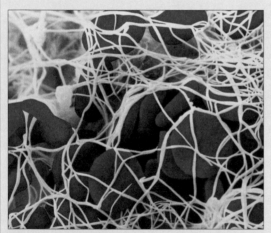

Red blood cells in a blood clot. The white material is strands of fibrin – the basis of the clot.

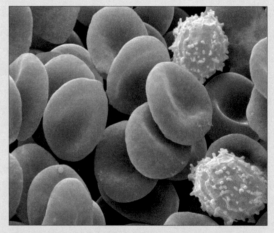

Two white blood cells in a sea of red blood cells. You can clearly see their different structure and shape.

White blood cells

These are the cells of defence and are fewer in number than red blood cells. There are two types: the phagocytes which eat disease organisms (microbes) and the lymphocytes which produce antibodies that act like chemical missiles against disease.

Platelets

These are tiny bodies in the blood that help to clot the blood. If the skin is damaged or cut this can let microbes in, so an emergency repair system quickly comes into action. Once a blood vessel is damaged the blood starts to leak out. When platelets come into contact with the air they break open. This causes a chain of reactions involving other chemicals in the blood (blood proteins) that leads to a clot forming in the damaged area.

Plasma

The other 60% of blood is a fluid called **plasma**. This is an almost colourless liquid (slightly yellow) that contains an enormous amount of substances such as:

• Water

• Dissolved food (glucose, amino acids, fats)

• Waste products (carbon dioxide, urea)

• Minerals

• Antibodies

• Blood clotting proteins

• Hormones

The bone marrow produces about 200 000 million red blood cells each day. Before a red blood cell dies it will have made about 172 000 journeys around the body. The blood vessels of the average adult would stretch almost $2\frac{1}{2}$ times around the Earth (about 95 000 km) if they were unravelled.

pigment = colouring

This is an extract from the first Sherlock Holmes novel, *A study in scarlet*, by Sir Arthur Conan Doyle. It was first published in 1887 and is narrated by Dr. Watson. This is the first time Dr. Watson has met Holmes, and they are introduced by Mr. Stamford.

This was a lofty chamber, lined and littered with countless bottles. Broad, low tables were scattered about, which bristled with retorts, test-tubes, and little Bunsen lamps, with their blue flickering flames. There was only one student in the room, who was bending over a distant table absorbed in his work. At the sound of our steps he glanced round and sprang to his feet with a cry of pleasure. "I've found it! I've found it," he shouted to my companion, running towards us with a test-tube in his hand. "I have found a re-agent which is precipitated by haemoglobin, and by nothing else." Had he discovered a gold mine, greater delight could not have shone upon his features.

"Dr. Watson, Mr. Sherlock Holmes," said Stamford, introducing us.

"How are you?" he said cordially, gripping my hand with a strength for which I should hardly have given him credit. "You have been in Afghanistan, I perceive."

"How on earth did you know that?" I asked in astonishment.

"Never mind," said he, chuckling to himself. "The question now is about haemoglobin. No doubt you see the significance of this discovery of mine?"

"It is interesting, chemically, no doubt," I answered, "but practically …"

"Why, man, it is the most practical medico-legal discovery for years. Don't you see that it gives us an infallible test for blood stains. Come over here now!" He seized me by the coat-sleeve in his eagerness, and drew me over to the table at which he had been working. "Let us have some fresh blood," he said, digging a long bodkin into his finger, and drawing off the resulting drop of blood in a chemical pipette. "Now, I add this small quantity of blood to a litre of water. You perceive that the resulting mixture has the appearance of pure water. The proportion of blood cannot be more than one in a million. I have no doubt, however, that we shall be able to obtain the characteristic reaction." As he spoke, he threw into the vessel a few white crystals, and then added some drops of a transparent fluid. In an instant the contents assumed a dull mahogany colour, and a brownish dust was precipitated to the bottom of the glass jar.

"Ha! ha!" he cried, clapping his hands, and looking as delighted as a child with a new toy. "What do you think of that?"

"It seems to be a very delicate test," I remarked.

"Beautiful! beautiful! The old Guiacum test was very clumsy and uncertain. So is the microscopic examination for blood corpuscles. The latter is valueless if the stains are a few hours old. Now, this appears to act as well whether the blood is old or new. Had this test been invented, there are hundreds of men now walking the earth who would long ago have paid the penalty of their crimes."

"Indeed!" I murmured.

"Criminal cases are continually hingeing upon that one point. A man is suspected of a crime months perhaps after it has been committed. His linen or clothes are examined, and brownish stains discovered upon them. Are they blood stains, or mud stains, or rust stains, or fruit stains, or what are they? That is a question which has puzzled many an expert, and why? Because there was no reliable test. Now we have the Sherlock Holmes' test, and there will no longer be any difficulty."

medico-legal = a combination of medical and legal evidence that can be used in law

infallible = something that cannot fail or be wrong

bodkin = a sharp instrument, a bit like a long pin

corpuscles = blood cells

1 In the section headed **Colour match**, why do staff at the National Blood Service centres look out for darker donations?

_____

_____

(1 mark)

2 Look again at the first paragraph, in the box. Explain why this has been placed at the beginning of the article.

_____

_____

_____

_____

_____

_____

_____

_____

(2 marks)

3 Look again at the information in the box. Why are the staff described as 'scientific'?

_____

_____

(1 mark)

4 This article also explains what can be learned from the colour of plasma:

Plasma is usually a clear yellow. However, it can look cloudy occasionally. This can be caused by a number of things. You could simply have eaten some fatty food before giving blood, or it could be caused by an underlying condition related to high fat content in the body. It may even indicate a problem with the donation with regard to bacteria.

    a How does the writer show that you cannot draw a direct conclusion from the colour of plasma?

_____

_____

_____

(2 marks)

b Why has the writer done this?

_____

_____

(1 mark)

5 The article is taken from a booklet sent to people registered as blood donors.
Why was the article included in the booklet?
You should comment on:
- The subject matter of the article
- The way it has been written
- The presentation and layout

_____

_____

_____

_____

_____

_____

_____

_____

_____

_____

_____

_____

_____

_____

_____

_____

_____

_____

_____

_____

_____

_____

(5 marks)

6 Why are platelets so important?

_____

(1 mark)

7 The information on these pages is intended to help GCSE students learn about Biology.
a Explain why each paragraph is given a heading and how this helps the reader of the textbook.

_____

_____

(1 mark)

b Explain why bullet points are used in the section headed **Plasma**, and how this helps the reader of the textbook.

_____

_____

(1 mark)

8 The writer has used brackets several times in this extract.
a Identify and write down an example of brackets being used.

_____

(1 mark)

b Explain why brackets are used in this way.

_____

_____

_____

(1 mark)

9 Why has this text been written? What is the writer trying to do?

_____

_____

_____

(1 mark)

10 How does the extract make this topic easy for the reader to follow?
You should comment on how the extract:
- Uses structural and layout devices
- Makes use of technical language and numbers
- Uses sentence structures.

_____

_____

_____

_____

_____

_____

_____

_____

_____

_____

_____

_____

_____

_____

_____

_____

_____

_____

_____

_____

_____

_____

_____

_____

_____

(5 marks)

11 What does Watson think of Holmes? Use a quotation to support your answer.

_____

_____

_____

_____

(2 marks)

12 Why does Holmes think his discovery is so important?

_____

_____

_____ (1 mark)

13 'This was a lofty chamber, lined and littered with countless bottles.'
What does the choice of language suggest about the room in which Holmes is working?

_____

_____

_____

_____ (2 marks)

14 What impression of Sherlock Holmes do you get from this extract?

_____

_____

_____

_____

_____

_____

_____

_____

_____

_____

_____

_____

(5 marks)

Writing skills

There's a lot more to being a great writer than just putting words in sentences and paragraphs!

Being a great writer means you are able to really think about what you are trying to say and how you are going to say it. There are lots of different sorts of writing and a great writer has to be able to be imaginative, interesting and thoughtful so their reader wants to read to the end, and sometimes even be left wanting more.

Great writers produce appropriate texts that are **organised** for greatest impact and can be followed by their readers. This includes features such as beautifully crafted sentences in logical and coherent paragraphs, and, of course, technical accuracy that includes spelling. Great writers also really think about their **vocabulary** and try to pick the best words – not necessarily the longest but the ones that do exactly what you want them to.

All of these features of a great writer have been broken down into different Assessment Focuses for KS3 and you will encounter them during your English lessons and in your Teacher Assessment at the end of Year 9.

Writing Assessment Focuses

AF1: write imaginative, interesting and thoughtful tasks
This means your work is interesting to read and shows your ideas.

AF2: produce texts which are appropriate to task, reader and purpose
This means your work is suitable for the intended audience, purpose and text type.

AF3: organise and present whole texts effectively, sequencing and structuring information, ideas and events
This means your ideas are easy to follow and develop in a logical way.

AF4: construct paragraphs and use cohesion within and between paragraphs
This means you use paragraphs and it is easy for the reader to see how each paragraph leads on to the next one. It is only assessed in the longer writing task.

AF5: vary sentences for clarity, purpose and effect
This means you construct your sentences to help convey your ideas. For example, you might use a very short simple sentence after a build-up of complex sentences to create contrast and impact.

AF6: write with technical accuracy of syntax and punctuation in phrases, clauses and sentences
Your word order is correct and your sentences say exactly what you want them to.

AF7: select appropriate and effective vocabulary
This means you choose carefully the best words for your writing.

AF8: use correct spelling
This is only assessed in the shorter writing task.

The tasks

This part of your KS3 English pack contains lots of different tasks for you to work through. Each task relates to the Assessment Focuses to ensure you practise all eight to be brilliant in your English lessons and your final Teacher Assessment.

It doesn't matter how long you spend on these tasks – in fact, it's better to take the time you need to make sure your answers are brilliant! To check your answers, turn to the back of the book.

When you get to the longer writing tasks you will need to work out the **purpose**, **audience** and **text type** before you start to plan. This will help you to work out exactly how to craft your response. It's really good to get into the habit of using this skill whenever you are reading or writing as it will help ensure you are great at both.

The writing questions all follow the same sort of format:

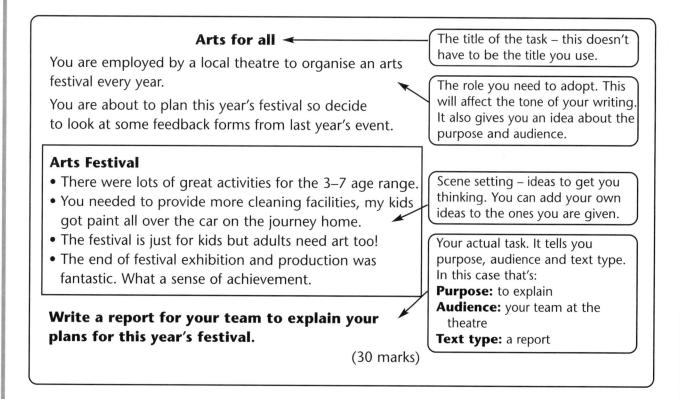

Arts for all
> *The title of the task – this doesn't have to be the title you use.*

You are employed by a local theatre to organise an arts festival every year.

You are about to plan this year's festival so decide to look at some feedback forms from last year's event.
> *The role you need to adopt. This will affect the tone of your writing. It also gives you an idea about the purpose and audience.*

Arts Festival
- There were lots of great activities for the 3–7 age range.
- You needed to provide more cleaning facilities, my kids got paint all over the car on the journey home.
- The festival is just for kids but adults need art too!
- The end of festival exhibition and production was fantastic. What a sense of achievement.

> *Scene setting – ideas to get you thinking. You can add your own ideas to the ones you are given.*

Write a report for your team to explain your plans for this year's festival.

(30 marks)

> *Your actual task. It tells you purpose, audience and text type. In this case that's:*
> **Purpose:** to explain
> **Audience:** your team at the theatre
> **Text type:** a report

Purpose, audience and text type

1 Read these text extracts and match each one to its intended audience and purpose (see opposite).

1 I wish to highlight the appalling state of the roads in my town. There are huge potholes which are not only uncomfortable but dangerous to all road users. Yesterday, I saw a cyclist fall off his bike after his front wheel went down one of these traps. Action is needed …

2 Good morning.

I would like to speak to you this morning about our need for proper cycle paths to school. We all know that cycling to school is fast and healthy, but only if we are not in danger from lorries and cars thundering past, threatening to knock us over.

Cycle paths could be our safe route to school, but we need to fight for them and that's where you come in …

3 Secondly, if the school were to provide safer cycle sheds more students would cycle to school, which would reduce the traffic around the school and make the roads safer for everyone. This is a benefit the school cannot ignore as it would also have a positive environmental impact …

4 Thank you for your interest in our Premium Cycle Sheds. I enclose a comprehensive brochure detailing the different models and options available and would like to draw your attention to the following points that make our product the market-leader:
- Value for money
- Designed to fit your school's needs
- Sturdy and secure
- Long-lasting and guaranteed for ten years

Our customers often find the best way to make a decision is with the help of one of our experts, and I am pleased to confirm that Lilly George will be happy to come and visit you to explain your options …

5 Issues with the Premium Cycle Shed

Claims on the ten year guarantee are high, with specific problems related to rust and corrosion. The cost to upgrade the materials to prevent this problem is roughly equal to the cost of repairs following claims. However, the increased product confidence and potential sales implication would make this route valuable.

Proposal

Upgrade materials ….

Intended audience

a Your head teacher
b Potential customer
c Your whole year group
d Project manager
e Local council members

Purpose (you might find the texts have more than one purpose)

i Persuade, argue, advise
ii Inform, explain, describe
iii Imagine, explore, entertain
iv Analyse, review, comment

Text	Intended audience	Purpose
1		
2		
3		
4		
5		

2 There are problems with these cycle sheds. Imagine you are the head teacher and you are not happy with the Premium Cycle Sheds you purchased for your school last year.

On a separate sheet of paper, write your letter of complaint to the company.

3 Now try identifying the **purpose, audience** and **text type** in this task.

Local radio star

You work as a radio presenter for your local radio station. You are going to the monthly meeting to suggest new ideas to make the radio station more interesting for young people in your area.
Your research has found the following:

Local radio for local teens
- Include information about local events for teenagers
- Have local teenage voices presenting – we don't want an adult telling us what to think
- Don't be afraid to raise difficult issues
- A good mix of new music, perhaps from local bands
- A review of gadgets and new stuff

ON AIR

Write a report to advise the radio station controller what to include in the new programme for teenagers.

Purpose _____

Audience _____

Text type _____

Using the right words

1 Amazing adjectives

Look at these adjectives. They can all be used to describe your tests.
Sort them into the correct column in the table.

> stimulating boring tedious essential exciting challenging
> interesting mundane ordinary dull normal wearisome
> vital crucial monotonous necessary commonplace usual

negative	neutral	positive
dull		

2 Vary your verbs

How many other words can you think of to replace these verbs?

a go _____

b said _____

c sleep _____

d cry _____

e walk _____

3 Use Standard English

How would you change these if you were giving a formal presentation?

a This product is really *cool*. _____

b I'll *catch* you later. _____

c I *dunno* what to suggest. _____

d *Hi ya!* _____

e We don't want to be *ripped off*. _____

4 Add some pictures

Can you think of any similes you can use to describe the following?

a a really fierce deputy head teacher _____

b a jolly and cheerful footballer _____

c a huge grey factory _____

d a small boat out at sea _____

e a child skiing down a mountain _____

5 Tug at the heart-strings

Can you change these phrases to make them more emotive?

a Young man hits old woman.

_____

b The Guildford Flames beat their opposition.

_____

c When the sun is shining I enjoy a cold drink.

_____

d We have to stay inside the house because there is too much snow around.

_____

e The old cat tried to catch a bird and failed.

_____

6 Know when to avoid bias

Can you change these emotive phrases into neutral ones?

a The bear ripped him to shreds.

_____

b The woodland was ravished by a terrifying blaze.

_____

c He shovelled the greasy burger into his mouth as if he was starved.

_____

d She shrieked as the thug yanked the handbag from her arm.

_____

e The crumbling school buildings are a death-trap.

_____

Sentence structures

1 Add some complexity

Re-write these extracts, changing the sentence structure to make them more powerful and coherent.

a I am very excited. I am going on holiday to America tomorrow. My whole family are going. What's really good is that I am allowed to take my best friend.

_____

_____

_____

b Cats are natural predators. When they see a bird or mouse it just means excitement to them. Sometimes they kill without the desire to eat their prey. Some cats can be shocked when they catch something.

_____

_____

_____

_____

2 Watch the length

These sentences are out of control. Re-write them, putting in punctuation to make the meaning clearer.

a The market was full of exciting smells and colours and noises and people and new things.

_____

_____

b Music can create the atmosphere you need to learn and it can even help you to remember ideas because when you come to revise you can listen to the same music and it will help you to recall the original idea because your memory has made a link.

_____

_____

_____

_____

_____

_____

3 Zoom into the action

Look at this sentence:

> In the shadows, under the stairs, resting against the chair was a bloody knife.

The reader is taken closer and closer to the really important discovery of the knife by the phrases that start the sentence.

Complete these sentences to zoom your reader into the action!

a At the end of the garden, beyond the tree was _____ .

b In the car, sitting quietly as directed, _____ .

c In the corner of the room, _____

_____ .

d Under the floorboards, _____

_____ .

4 Add layers of meaning

A complex sentence has a main clause and one or more subordinate clauses:

> They ate chocolates greedily, until they felt sick.

The main clause, 'They ate chocolates greedily' can be understood by itself but the subordinate clause, 'until they felt sick' doesn't make sense by itself.

Underline the main clause in red and the subordinate clause in blue, in these sentences.

a I hid under the duvet shaking, as the storm raged outside.

b Claire, who was filled with a sense of relief, left the stage.

c Until the power cut hit, Paul refused to leave his computer.

Re-write these as complex sentences. You might choose to put the subordinate clause at the beginning, in the middle or at the end.

d Sally loved the book. She missed her bus because she was reading it. _____

_____

e The computer finally died. It had been used non-stop. _____

_____

f Amanda bought some new pink shoes. She loved shopping. _____

_____

Paragraphs and structure

1 Read this extract and mark where the paragraphs should go. You might want to change the order.

When you first see my house you might think it's a bit dull and dingy because there are plants growing up the front wall and the path is a bit overgrown. I like to think this adds character and makes it more exciting when you come and visit me. If I trust you, and the others say it's OK, I might take you to the end of the garden to see our den. It's taken us years to create it and it's simply the best place to be in the summer. Once you are in you'll probably be drawn into the kitchen as there's generally something good cooking and that's where we tend to be. It's funny really, as it's the smallest room in the house but it's where we spend our time together. (Well, not the smallest, but you wouldn't all sit round the bathroom to talk about the day, would you?) Stepping through the front door for the first time is normally a bit of a shock because we've painted the inside really bright colours. The woodwork (that's the doors and skirting boards) is pink and the walls are purple. My gran hates it, but we sat down and made a family decision so it's fine by us.

2 You also need to start new paragraphs when there's a new speaker. Mark the paragraph breaks in this extract with a forward slash (/).

"Look, I'm really sorry," said Barry with frustration, "but this is just not going to work and that's an end to it." He threw down the play script and stood up to go. Laura looked up at him. "I'm really sorry as well," she said with sarcasm, "I'm really sorry that we've wasted so much time rehearsing with you in the lead role when we could have had Lance. He would at least have listened to our ideas." "That's just typical, " replied Barry, "and that's why I'm leaving. You've never wanted me in this stupid play. Well, if you think Lance will have anything to do with you when he hears how you've treated me you've got another think coming!" The rest of the cast sat watching with amazement as he coolly collected his jacket and walked out of the rehearsal room. Laura sat stunned. "Did that really just happen?" she asked, "Did we finally get rid of that idiot?" "Yes!" shouted Sian with joy. "Well done, you finally did it!"

3 Choose the appropriate connectives from the list and add them to the recipe below.

| Next | Finally | Then | Secondly | Firstly |

_____ pre-heat the oven to 180°.

_____ take your vegetables and chop them into 1 cm size cubes.

_____ lightly oil the baking tray and arrange the vegetables on it so they are evenly spaced.

_____ put the tray in the oven and set the timer to 40 minutes.

_____ remove the vegetables from the oven and enjoy!

Writing in different formats

1 Look at the text types in the box and the list of writing elements below. Match the most likely text type (or types) to each element.

| letter   newspaper   story   leaflet   report   speech |

- Your address in the top right

  _____

- Impersonal phrases

  _____

- The date

  _____

- Snappy headline

  _____

- Alliteration

  _____

- Short paragraphs

  _____

- Bullet points

  _____

- Sign-off of 'Yours faithfully, Yours sincerely' or a more informal phrase if you know the person

  _____

- Rhetorical techniques

  _____

- Entertain and inform

  _____

- Informal style

  _____

- Repetition

  _____

- Clear but lively

  _____

- Factual

  _____

- Formal address

  _____

- Short sentences

  _____

- Clear statement of purpose

  _____

- Sub-heading

  _____

- Modal verbs

  _____

- Emotive language

  _____

- Personal pronouns

  _____

- The address of the person you are writing to in the top left

  _____

- Formal style

  _____

- Quotations from experts

  _____

- Pattern of three

  _____

- Varied length of sentences

  _____

2 Label these features in the newspaper article below.

headline   sub-heading   use of expert   illustration   caption

PET FISH FRIED
Fish lover left red-faced

Paul Roberts, fish owning expert, was left red-faced yesterday, after he managed to fry hundreds of pounds worth of Koi Carp.

Roberts, who travels the world advising on the care of these creatures, fitted his own water filter system, something he advises his readers to leave to the professionals.

Unfortunately, he made a fatal error with the wiring and managed to heat his pond to near-tropical temperatures! The poor fish didn't stand a chance, as their home boiled and then exploded.

The stone pond exploded under the pressure of the boiling water and the boiled carp were sent flying. "My cat thought it was wonderful as cooked fish came flying through the air" explained Roberts' neighbour, Brian Downing, "although it was a horrendous noise!"

Roberts wasn't available for comment, but his wife said he was shocked and very saddened.

£400 Koi cat food

3 Now find these features in the speech below.

emotive language   repetition   alliteration   list of three

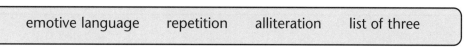

"Everybody knows that litter is dirty and dangerous. So why do we just drop our litter?

Rats are attracted to places with lots of litter, such as our school. Now, you might have an idea of rats as cute and cuddly, but they actually spread dangerous diseases such as cholera, typhus and leptospirosis. We do not want these around our school, so why do we just drop our litter?

We need to make a stand. We need to make a difference. You need to make a difference.

Firstly, take responsibility for your own actions. Put your litter in a bin or your bag.

Secondly, take responsibility for our community. Challenge anyone you see dropping litter. Explain what the consequences could be and ask them to put their litter in a bin.

Finally, if you see a piece of litter, don't walk over it: deal with it. By doing this you will make a difference. "

Punctuation

1 Write these sentences correctly.

a i am going to the shop to buy some crisps my dog needs to walk

_____

_____

b the shopping centre banned teenagers as they were bad news they thought

_____

_____

c james and amanda are going to france to learn to ski i hope they enjoy it

_____

_____

d i can't believe top of the pops is still going after all these years it's really amazing

_____

_____

e my english teacher is going to be really impressed with my improved writing skills

_____

_____

2 Use commas, dashes, colons, semi-colons and brackets to improve these sentences.

a You will need a pen a pencil and a ruler.

_____

b I had a great birthday thanks.

_____

c Jane likes Shakespeare Caroline prefers modern drama.

_____

d The bread which was actually put out for the birds had been eaten by the cat.

_____

_____

3 Shorten these words using an apostrophe.

a I am   _____

b it is   _____

c they are _____

d you are _____

e we are   _____

4 Remove the apostrophe from these words and write them out in full.

a he's   _____

b let's   _____

c could've _____

d can't   _____

e we've   _____

5 Re-write these sentences using an apostrophe to show ownership.

a The cats which belonged to Lucy were hungry.

_____

b Let's all go round to the flat belonging to Wayne for a party.

_____

c I won all the prizes at the sports day belonging to my school.

_____

d The provision for young people provided by my town is inadequate.

_____

e The car belonging to my brother is a heap of junk.

_____

Spelling

1 Plurals

Change these words into plurals.

a bus   _buses_

b try   _____

c potato   _____

d church   _____

e child   _____

f sheep   _____

g fox   _____

h car   _____

i tomato   _____

j business   _____

k calf   _____

l rush   _____

2 Present to past

Write the present participle and past tense of these verbs.

a to run   _running_   _ran_

b to stop   _____   _____

c to drop   _____   _____

d to decide   _____   _____

e to watch   _____   _____

f to form   _____   _____

g to admit   _____   _____

h to prefer   _____   _____

i to benefit   _____   _____

j to state   _____   _____

k to fight   _____   _____

l to begin   _____   _____

3 Misspellings

Write these words correctly.

a acomodation _____

b asessment _____

c audince _____

d buisness _____

e embarase _____

f explaination _____

g intresting _____

h marrage _____

i peple _____

j recieve _____

k secondery _____

l seperate _____

m sincerly _____

n serprise _____

o tommorow _____

p wierd _____

4 Beware of homophones

Underline the correct word in these sentences.

a Lance and Susan are looking forward to **they're / there / their** holiday.

b "**Who's / Whose** homework is this?" asked the teacher. "It doesn't have a name!"

c The old house was very creepy at night because it was so **quiet / quite**.

d "You may all go to lunch **accept / except** Katie."

e You need to explain the **effect / affect** of the metaphor.

f Oh, look! My pen is over **they're / there / their**.

g "**Who's / Whose** up for swimming?" asked Andrea.

h I was **quiet / quite** pleased with my homework but the teacher didn't seem impressed.

i I've got to go up in assembly to **accept / except** a prize on behalf of my tutor group.

Writing to review: shorter writing task

Poor Luke!

You receive the following email from a friend who is recovering in hospital following an operation.

New Message

| Send | New | Attach | Find | Font | Print |

To:

Subject:

Hello there, thanks for your last email. I think I would die of boredom without your emails. I can't believe I'm only allowed to use the computer for half an hour a day! Oh well, got to share it, I suppose.

I'm having to spend time reading now, and I'm really getting into it. Have you read any good books or seen any good films lately? I'd love to hear about something you think I should read or watch.

Right, got to go now. I look forward to hearing from you!

All the best

Luke

> Don't forget you have to use Standard English, even though this is an email to a friend.

Write an email to Luke in which you review a book or film you think he will enjoy.

(20 marks including 4 marks for spelling)

> You are not provided with a planning sheet for the shorter writing task but you still need to plan!

Writing to comment: shorter writing task

Be the spokesperson!

Your school has conducted a survey to see if its students want to keep or change their school uniform.

Here are the results:

17% of students don't want any kind of uniform.

20% of students want to keep the current uniform.

63% of students want to keep a uniform, but not the current one.

– Of these, the majority want a more varied uniform.

– There is also much support for the idea that Years 10 and 11 have a slightly different uniform from Years 7–9.

The sixth form don't want a uniform at all.

The head teacher would like you to comment on these results so that the Leadership Team know what action to take.

Write your commentary on these results.

(20 marks including 4 marks for spelling)

You are not provided with a planning sheet for the shorter writing task but you still need to plan!

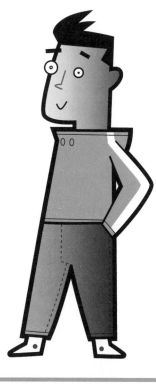

Writing to describe: shorter writing task

Celebrating past lives

Older people can be inspiring, interesting, scary or a mixture of all these things.

- What have they seen/experienced?

- How has this affected them today?

- What do you think about them?

Think about an old person you know or have heard about, and write a detailed description of them.

(20 marks including 4 marks for spelling)

You are not provided with a planning sheet for the shorter writing task but you still need to plan!

Writing to explain: shorter writing task

Holiday decisions

Your family is trying to decide where to go on holiday.
You have found the following holiday:

Family favourite

Join us at Glowing Sands for the family holiday of a
lifetime. There's so much to do, for all the family:

- **Relaxation zone** – calm and tranquil, for those chill-out
  times
- **Music zone** – live music, karaoke and the club. Music
  and performance lessons are available; who knows,
  maybe you'll be on the stage at the end of the week?
- **Art zone** – think, look, create. Express the artist in you.
- **Beauty zone** – pamper your body and make sure it's a
  whole new you at the end of the week.
- **Nature zone** – for those who like to get out and about –
  the beauty of our natural setting awaits. From nature
  walks, to getting to grips with your gardening.
- **Sea zone** – develop your skills on the sea. Windsurfing,
  sailing and diving are all available.

Decide if you would like to go on this holiday or not.

Write your ideas down to explain them.

(20 marks including 4 marks for spelling)

> You are not provided
> with a planning sheet
> for the shorter writing
> task but you still need
> to plan!

Writing fiction: Longer writing task

New worlds, new experiences

You are writing a story about the first landing on a new planet.

Your characters have been travelling in space for over a year and have finally landed on this new planet.

Below are some notes you have made for the next chapter of this novel.

Notes for chapter about landing on Planet X

Include:

- How the characters feel after travelling for over a year
- Worries and concerns they have about what is about to happen
- Their first reaction to Planet X

Character notes:

- Ann is a 'get up and go' sort of person. She has found the journey really difficult.
- Afsheen is impatient to explore Planet X.
- Mark is very aware of the possible dangers of a new planet.

Write the next chapter of the novel.

(30 marks)

You may wish to use this page to plan your work.

(This page will not be marked.)

Don't forget to identify purpose, audience, text type!

- Notes about the journey and how the astronauts feel

- The conversation they have and the decisions they make before getting out

- The new planet – what they can see, hear, smell, taste, touch

- What happens when they get out of the spacecraft

Use lined paper to write your answer. You can assess your work by checking the sample levelled answers at the back of this book.

Writing to describe: Longer writing task

Local descriptions of local places

Your English teacher gives you the following and suggests you take part:

Local writers wanted to describe local places

WE NEED YOU!

We're publishing a new guide to the UK, but this time the entries are to be by people who really know their places. Rather than sending travel writers to visit your town for half a day and then write about it, we want to get the truth.

Write an entry for our new guidebook and you could see your work in our new book!

You will need to cover the following areas, but we want your description to be as interesting as possible:

• The setting and atmosphere

• Local life – what's going on there?

• The best bits

• Things that need to be changed

• Your overall impression.

Write a description of the place where you live, to enter the competition.

(30 marks)

You may wish to use this page to plan your work.

(This page will not be marked.)

Don't forget to identify purpose, audience, text type!

• What does it look like, what can you see? What is the atmosphere like?

• Local events – what is there to do?

• The good things about living here

• The bad things about living here

• What I think of the place where I live.

Use lined paper to write your answer. You can assess your work by checking the sample levelled answers at the back of this book.

Writing to inform: Longer writing task

The next stages of my life ...

You have received a letter from a relative you don't see very often. Here is part of it:

I enjoyed reading about your school play and am sorry I wasn't able to come and see you. I am really pleased it went so well.

I do enjoy reading about your school life. I know it must be boring for you to have to write about it, but school seems so different from when I was there (I don't want to admit how many years ago that was). What else is happening there?

Write a letter to this relative telling them about your school life.
Do not include an address.

You might like to use one or more of the following ideas:

• Your option choices for Year 10

• Your extra-curricular activities

• Your lessons

• How your school day is organised

(30 marks)

You may wish to use this page to plan your work.

(This page will not be marked.)

Don't forget to identify purpose, audience, text type!

- Ideas to open the letter and my response to the letter I was sent

Ideas to include in reply

• The decisions I've had to make about my options	• The decisions I made and my reasons	• The events and changes I'm looking forward to

Use lined paper to write your answer. You can assess your work by checking the sample levelled answers at the back of this book.

Writing to review: Longer writing task

Music with you all day long ...

You work for a magazine that reviews electrical gadgets. You have been sent a new revolutionary music player to review. Here are the specifications:

MusicWrap

At last, a music player that doesn't need wires!

Key specifications:

- It looks like a wristwatch and tells the time, but it also plays music!

- You can download up to 10,000 tracks onto it.

- The music quality is second to none.

- It's wrapped round your wrist so you won't lose it!

- You don't need wires! Wireless technology means you just clip the headphones to your ears.

- Easy to use, fabulous to listen to!

Write the review for your magazine.

(30 marks)

You may wish to use this page to plan your work.

(This page will not be marked.)

Don't forget to identify purpose, audience, text type!

- What do you think of the idea?

- How does the wristwatch player work? Benefits? Problems?

- How do the wireless headphones work? Benefits? Problems?

- Would you recommend it?

Use lined paper to write your answer. You can assess your work by checking the sample levelled answers at the back of this book.

Supermarket threat

You read this article in your local paper:

Skate threat from supermarket

Local planning officers were considering a planning application from a large supermarket yesterday. Foods 'R'Us has applied to build a new store where the skatepark currently is.

Although the store will provide lots of jobs and be very useful for local people there is already some opposition to it.

Local shopkeepers are worried their small shops will go out of business and local kids want to know where they are supposed to go if their skatepark disappears.

Planning officers have raised these issues with Foods 'R'Us and are awaiting their reply. In the meantime, they have asked local people to let them know what they think. Write to …

Write a letter to the planning officer to advise them what to do.
Do not include an address.

(30 marks)

You may wish to use this page to plan your work.

(This page will not be marked.)

Don't forget to identify purpose, audience, text type!

Advantages of the new supermarket being built

- More convenient shopping

- More jobs

Disadvantages of the new supermarket being built

- Loss of the skatepark

- Loss of local businesses

Use lined paper to write your answer. You can assess your work by checking the sample levelled answers at the back of this book.

Practice writing paper

Have a go at answering this practice writing paper.

Make sure you are in a quiet place and can spend 1 hour 15 minutes without being disturbed.

You need to keep an eye on the time so that you spend 45 minutes on the longer writing task and 30 minutes on the shorter writing task.

- Spend 15 minutes reading and planning the longer writing task. You are given a planning sheet. Although you don't *have* to use it, it does make sense to do so.

- Spend 25 minutes writing your answer to the longer writing task. This leaves you 5 minutes to go through checking, correcting and improving your work.

- Spend 10 minutes reading and planning the shorter writing task. Although you are not given a planning sheet, you still need to make a plan.

- Remember to spend 5 minutes going through and checking, correcting and improving your answer to this task.

Writing paper

Longer writing task

This is worth 30 marks and you should spend 45 minutes on it.

Shorter writing task

This is worth 20 marks, including 4 marks for spelling. You should spend 30 minutes on it.

You will need separate paper to answer these tasks.

Longer writing task

Money matters

You have just received the following information from the school governors:

> The governors are delighted to announce that Liz Day, a past student, has made a gift of £10,000 to the school.
>
> The governors would like to know what you, the students, think this money should be spent on. Some suggestions are listed below, or you can make your own suggestion:
>
> • Use the money to buy new computer equipment.
>
> • Buy new books for the library.
>
> • Spend it on a school visit for the whole school.
>
> • Build a statue of Miss Day to express thanks.
>
> • Develop the school's sports facilities.
>
> • Buy new musical instruments.

Write a letter to the governors to persuade them to spend the money on the project of your choice.

(30 marks)

Longer writing task

Planning page

You can use this page to make notes for your letter.

(This page will not be marked.)

• What should the money be spent on?	• Why is this a good project?
• Why is this better than other ideas?	• How will it benefit the whole school?

Shorter writing task

Teen TV

You receive a memo from your boss:

I've just received this data from our research team. It looks like we need a new programme for teenagers – to fill the 4–4.30 slot.

Have a look at the data and let me have your ideas as quickly as possible, please.

Research into new teenage show:

We need something new for 4–4.30.

- This is prime time for the teen market – they are home and could be in front of the TV.

- There was a positive response to the following content:
  - Live music
  - Magazine style
  - Fast competitions, for viewers to win something substantial

- There was a negative response to the following content:
  - Silly games
  - Adult presenters behaving like children
  - Competitions for studio guests

Our competitors fill this slot with cartoons, programmes aimed at the younger market and talk shows for adults We want a programme for the 13–16 audience.

What do you think? Write an outline of a TV programme that might be suitable for this audience and time slot.

(20 marks including 4 marks for spelling)

Reading and writing checklist

Reading

I am able to:

- Understand texts and find information in them ☐
- Describe what happens in a text ☐
- Select information to support my ideas ☐
- Provide quotations to support my ideas ☐
- Deduce and infer ideas from texts ☐
- Interpret texts to explain what an author means or wants us to think ☐
- Identify structural features such as connectives used to direct the reader ☐
- Explain how a text has been organised to direct the reader ☐
- Comment on presentation ☐
- Explain how writers have used language ☐
- Identify and explain writers' word choices ☐
- Identify and explain how writers have used techniques such as:
  - repetition ☐
  - rhetorical questions ☐
  - alliteration ☐
  - metaphor ☐
  - simile ☐
- Identify features that show what a writer's purpose is ☐
- Comment on a writer's purpose and viewpoint ☐
- Comment on the overall effect of the text on the reader ☐

Writing

I am able to:

- Write clearly and accurately, so my writing is easy to follow ☐
- Develop my writing in a thoughtful way ☐
- Match my writing to the intended audience ☐
- Match my writing to the purpose ☐
- Organise my writing so it makes sense and develops logically ☐
- Sequence my ideas for maximum impact on my reader ☐
- Write in clear paragraphs ☐
- Write in paragraphs that develop logically and make sense ☐
- Link my paragraphs using connectives ☐
- Use simple, compound and complex sentences to create maximum impact on my reader ☐
- Vary my sentences for clarity and purpose ☐
- Punctuate my sentences accurately ☐
- Choose appropriate and effective vocabulary ☐
- Use my imagination to write interesting texts ☐
- Use correct spelling ☐

Shakespeare skills

Your English lessons aren't just about Reading and Writing – you will also cover Literature.

There are some amazing authors published in English, but perhaps the most famous is Shakespeare and everyone studies him in KS3 and KS4. It's a great idea to learn how to read and write about Shakespeare now as you'll have to do it for GCSE in KS4. More importantly, it's good to study Shakespeare because his plays and poems are really, really good!

Shakespeare wrote 37 plays and hundreds of poems. We've focused on the plays here because you have to study one during KS3. The skills you learn from studying a Shakespeare play will help you with your reading, writing and study of all Literature texts.

Literature can appear to be complicated when you start to study it, so it's a good idea to break it down into different areas of focus. We have used four different areas in this section:

• **Character and motivation**
This means you have to understand the behaviour of the main characters. You need to know and explain why the characters behave as they do.

• **Ideas, themes and issues**
This means that you have to understand the particular ideas (such as love or revenge) that your play explores.

• **The language of the text**
This means looking at what Shakespeare's characters say, how they say it and the effect this has on the audience.

• **The text in performance**
This means understanding and explaining how the scenes would have been performed, and how you might put them on if you were the director.

You'll find a combination of tasks that help you to unpick and understand different aspects of the play you are studying. If the example isn't from your play, don't worry because the tasks can be completed for any play.

You'll also find tasks focused on the language. Lots of people find this a bit daunting, but take your time and try to say it aloud – that really can help to work out the exact meaning. When you are analysing the language try to be as specific as possible and don't be afraid to write down any ideas the words create for you.

The longer tasks are all organised in the same way and have been written to allow you to answer them no matter which play you are studying:

Shakespeare question ← You will need to think about the play you have studied.

Key scenes: _____

← Your teacher will probably focus your lessons on some key scenes that you will study in detail. Make sure you know what these are before your Teacher Assessment and that you have a copy of them as you work through this section.

_____

In these extracts, how is the idea of power explored through the main character?

← Obviously you know who your main character is!

Support your ideas by referring to both of the extracts which are printed on the following pages. ←

It's a really good idea to refer to and quote from more than one key scene as this shows greater knowledge and understanding of the whole play.

(18 marks)

Preparing for the Shakespeare test

1 Fill in the information:

The play I am studying: —————————————————————————

The key scenes I am studying: —————————————————————

The main characters in those scenes: ————————————————

2 Character development

Look at the graph for your play. Track how each key character changes on this emotion graph. Use a different colour for each character to make it clear. You already have one character's changing emotions shown, to start you off.

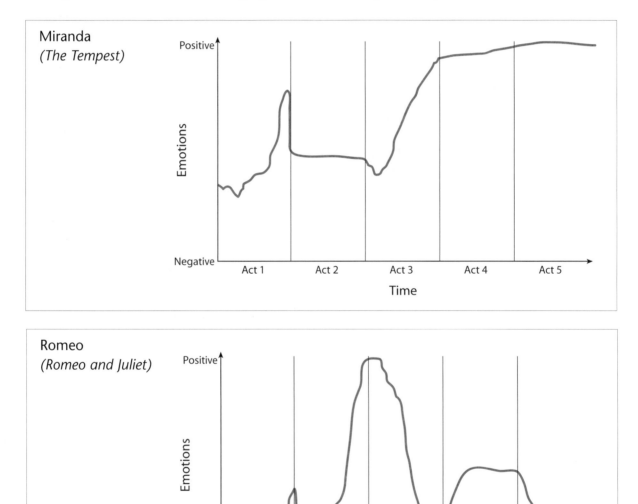

Miranda
(The Tempest)

Romeo
(Romeo and Juliet)

3 Character analysis

Many characters in Shakespeare's plays are like icebergs – they don't show everyone what they are really like. Complete an 'iceberg' for each of your main characters.

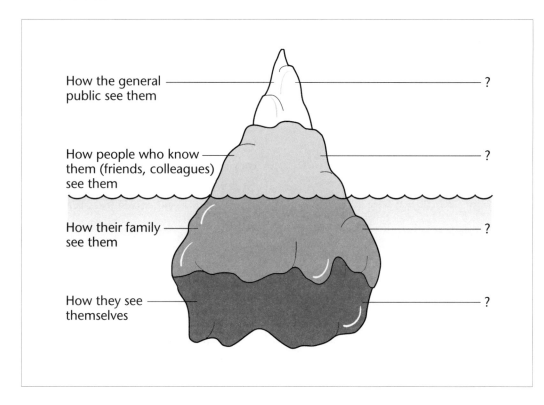

Try to find quotations to support your ideas at each level.

4 Understanding the scenes

You've focused on the characters; now think about the way Shakespeare has structured the scenes. Fill in this tension graph for each of your key scenes.

Shakespeare's language

The Tempest

1 Match the meanings

Draw lines to match the modern English versions with these quotations.

Shakespeare's words	Modern version
1 The fringèd curtains of thine eye advance, And say what thou see'st yond.	**A** I am chattering without control and forgetting my father's commands to ignore you.
2 Most sure the goddess On whom these airs attend!	**B** As soon as I saw you I fell in love with you and my heart became yours, to serve you. As my heart is still with you, I am slave to you. Therefore I will move logs without complaint.
3 But I prattle Something too wildly, and my father's precepts I therein do forget.	**C** Open your eyes, with their lashes that act as a fringe to the curtain of your eyelids, and say what you see before you.
4 The very instant that I saw you, did My heart fly to your service – there resides, To make me slave to it – and for your sake Am I this patient log-man.	**D** You must be the goddess that this music is played for

2 Analyse the language

Look at the quotations below. For each one, identify the language technique that has been used and explain the effect it has. The first one has been done for you.

> alliteration   metaphor   simile

Quotation	Technique	Effect
'the wild waves whist	alliteration of 'w'	Reflects the movement of the waves and spray.
'the fringèd curtains of thine eye'		
'thou shalt be as free / As mountain winds'		
'Poor worm, thou art infected!'		
'But you – o you, So perfect and so peerless – are created Of every creature's best'		

Romeo and Juliet

1 Match the meanings

Draw lines to match the modern English versions with these quotations.

Shakespeare's words	Modern version
1 Who set this ancient quarrel new abroach? Speak, nephew. Where you by when it began?	**A** Why does a name matter? What does a name mean? The flower we call a rose would still smell sweet if it had a different name.
2 So early walking did I see your son. Towards him I made, be he was ware of me, And stole into the covert of the wood.	**B** Don't swear by the moon because it changes every month. If you do, your love might also change all the time.
3 What's in a name? That which we call a rose By any other name would smell as sweet.	**C** Who started this old argument up again? Nephew, did you see it start? Tell me what happened.
4 O swear not by the moon, th' inconstant moon, That monthly changes in her circled orb, Lest that thy love prove likewise variable.	**D** I saw your son when I was out walking really early one morning. I went towards him, but he was aware of me and went into the wood where he was hidden from sight.

2 Analyse the language

Look at the quotations below. For each one, identify the language technique that has been used and explain the effect it has. The first one has been done for you.

> alliteration   oxymoron   metaphor   assonance

Quotation	Technique	Effect
'the bud bit with an envious worm'	alliteration of 'b'	Reflects the harsh and secret way the worm has infected the bud.
'O brawling love, O loving hate'		
'What light through yonder window breaks? It is the east, and Juliet is the sun'		
'love's light wings'		
'Love goes toward love as schoolboys from their books'		

Character and motivation

Choose the question that relates to the play you are studying. Use the space under the question to make notes and to write your plan. Write your actual answer on lined paper.

For more practice, you could have a go at answering the question(s) on the other play. Just substitute the name of the character.

The Tempest

Focus on the key scenes of your play.

What impression do you get of Miranda in these scenes?

Support your ideas by referring to **at least two** of the scenes you have studied in detail.

(18 marks)

The Tempest

Focus on the key scenes of your play.

What impression do you get of Ferdinand in these scenes?

Support your ideas by referring to **at least two** of the scenes you have studied in detail.

(18 marks)

Romeo and Juliet

Focus on the key scenes of your play.

How does Romeo change in these scenes?

Support your ideas by referring to **at least two** of the scenes you have studied in detail.

(18 marks)

Themes

Choose the question that relates to the play you are studying. Use the space under the question to make notes and to write your plan. Write your actual answer on lined paper.

For more practice, you could have a go at answering the question(s) on the other play. Just substitute the theme.

The Tempest

Focus on the key scenes of your play.

How is the theme of love explored in these scenes?

Support your ideas by referring to **at least two** of the scenes you have studied in detail.

(18 marks)

Romeo and Juliet

Focus on the key scenes of your play.

How is the theme of love explored in these scenes?

Support your ideas by referring to **at least two** of the scenes you have studied in detail.

(18 marks)

Romeo and Juliet

Focus on the key scenes of your play.

How is the idea of deception explored in these scenes?

Support your ideas by referring to **at least two** of the scenes you have studied in detail.

(18 marks)

Language

Choose the question that relates to the play you are studying. Use the space under the question to make notes and to write your plan. Write your actual answer on lined paper.

For more practice, you could have a go at answering the question(s) on the other play. Just substitute the name of the character.

Top Tip!

Make sure you explain the impact key words and phrases have on our understanding, and use really short quotations as evidence to show you know the exact words that are having the effect.

The Tempest

Focus on the key scenes of your play.

The language used in these scenes emphasises the high emotions experienced by the characters. Explain how Shakespeare has used the language to create this emotion.

Support your ideas by referring to **at least two** of the scenes you have studied in detail.

(18 marks)

Romeo and Juliet

Focus on the key scenes of your play.

Romeo and Juliet both play with language. Explain how Shakespeare uses language to show they are a good match.

Support your ideas by referring to **at least two** of the scenes you have studied in detail.

(18 marks)

Romeo and Juliet

Focus on the key scenes of your play.

Romeo's language is used to create his personality. Explain how Shakespeare does this.

Support your ideas by referring to **at least two** of the scenes you have studied in detail.

(18 marks)

The text in performance

Choose the question that relates to the play you are studying. Use the space under the question to make notes and to write your plan. Write your actual answer on lined paper.

For more practice, you could have a go at answering the question(s) on the other play. Just substitute the name of the character.

Don't forget, this is **not** about saying you want an actor to 'move to the front of the stage and look upset' – it is focused on **language**, not movement.

The Tempest

Focus on the key scenes of your play.

Ferdinand's emotions change dramatically in this play. Imagine you are directing this play. Explain how you want the actor playing Ferdinand to show his thoughts and emotions in these scenes.

Support your ideas by referring to **at least two** of the scenes you have studied in detail.

(18 marks)

The Tempest

Focus on the key scenes of your play.

The relationship between Prospero and Miranda is very important. Imagine you are directing this play and explain how you want the actors playing these characters to show their thoughts and emotions in these scenes.

Support your ideas by referring to **at least two** of the scenes you have studied in detail.

(18 marks)

Romeo and Juliet

Focus on the key scenes of your play.

Romeo's emotions change dramatically in this play. Imagine you are directing this play and explain how you want the actor playing Romeo to show his thoughts and emotions in these scenes.

Support your ideas by referring to **at least two** of the scenes you have studied in detail.

(18 marks)

Practice Shakespeare paper

Try this practice Shakespeare paper.

Make sure you are in a quiet place and can spend 45 minutes without being disturbed.

You need to keep an eye on the time so that you spend 10 minutes planning, 30 minutes writing your answer and 5 minutes checking and improving.

- You will need your copy of the key scenes.

- You will also need a pen and lined paper.

Shakespeare paper

This is worth 18 marks and you should spend 45 minutes on it.

This paper contains one task and you should answer it with reference to the key scenes of the Shakespeare play you have studied.

Answer the task that relates to the play you have studied.

The Tempest

Focus on the key scenes of your play.

Miranda's emotions change dramatically in this play. Imagine you are directing this play and explain how you want the actor playing Miranda to show her thoughts and emotions in these scenes.

Support your ideas by referring to **at least two** of the scenes you have studied in detail.

(18 marks)

Romeo and Juliet

Focus on the key scenes of your play.

What impression do you get of Romeo in these scenes?

Support your ideas by referring to **at least two** of the scenes you have studied in detail.

(18 marks)

You may use this page to plan your answer.

Shakespeare checklist

I am able to:

- Understand the events in the play ☐

- Understand the characters and their motivations ☐

- Describe what happens in my set scenes ☐

- Select key quotations to support my ideas ☐

- Make specific references to events in the play ☐

- Deduce and infer ideas from the events in the play ☐

- Identify structural features that add to the meaning of the play ☐

- Comment on stagecraft ☐

- Explain and comment on Shakespeare's use of language, including: ☐

   – metaphor ☐

   – simile ☐

   – alliteration ☐

   – onomatopoeia ☐

   – imagery ☐

   – repetition ☐

   – symbol ☐

- Explain the impact the text has on the audience ☐

Notes

Notes

Reading answers

pages 100–101

Purpose = to describe the setting and introduce the character
Audience = teenage readers of the book
Text type = prose, descriptive fiction writing

1 *Any one of:*

   • 'Matt heard it and looked up briefly.'
   • 'the crowd meant nothing to him.'
   • 'He wasn't part of it.'
   (1 mark)

2 The writer emphasises Matt's isolation by starting and ending the extract with a description of him by himself. The first sentence is actually a paragraph of its own, which makes it more of a striking statement. The final descriptions of him at the end of the extract are firstly a short statement and then a broken sentence. This sandwiching effect is contrasted with the chaos and confusion that is going on around him. The busy street is juxtaposed with Matt as an individual and helps to make him seem different and apart from it.
   (2 marks, one each for any two of the above points)

3

Example of descriptive language	The impression it gives
'commuters were fighting their way out of the station.'	This gives the impression of pressure and chaos.
' a tangle of cars, taxis and pedestrians'.	Everything seems confused and busy.
' Somebody leant on their horn and the noise blared out'	The noise seems loud and ugly.

(1 mark for each up to a maximum of 2 marks)

4 Matt is made to seem isolated by the way he is set apart from the rest of the world and the language that has been used. The structure of the piece emphasises his isolation – he is described at the beginning and end of the extract and this description is juxtaposed with the busy commuter scene. Secondly, we are told he doesn't really react to what is going on around him, even though it is noisy and chaotic: 'Matt heard it and looked up briefly'. This suggests he is in a world of his own. Finally, we are told that the world around him is 'fighting' and a 'tangle' but he is just 'sitting'. This lack of movement makes him seem different and therefore isolated.
   (3 marks. Notice there are three main points made. You would get a mark per point you make.)

5 It is clear that something bad is going to happen because we are told Matt knows he is 'making a mistake'. Perhaps he is going to do something that goes against the law or society. He is shown as being isolated, which suggests he does not feel like he is part of society, so maybe he doesn't care about doing something bad.
   (2 marks)

pages 102–103

Purpose = to describe and entertain
Audience = teenage/adult readers of the book
Text type = prose, descriptive fiction writing

1 He is being told what to do by someone who has no right to do so.
   (1 mark)

2 *Any two of:*
   • 'narrowed his eyes'
   • 'wished he were taller, stronger and eight years older'
   • 'a ball of anger exploded inside him'
   • 'made him wish he had the courage to say exactly what he wanted to say'
   (1 mark)

3

Quotation	What it tells us about Bruno's state of mind
'Bruno narrowed his eyes and wished he were taller, stronger and eight years older'	Bruno is in a confrontational mood and wants to be as big, strong and old as the person he is angry with so that he can taken them on.
'A ball of anger exploded inside him'	This suggests a powerful knot of anger has been building up but it has now been let loose.

(1 mark each)

1

4 He doesn't like the Lieutenant telling him what to do and thinks he has no right to. He has very little respect for the Lieutenant, as shown by the sneering way he refers to his title as a 'fancy title'.
(1 mark)

5 Bruno is made to seem young by his use of the proper nouns 'Mother' and 'Father'. The fact he has not abbreviated them shows he is doing exactly as he is told and does not think of his parents in any way other than their relationship to him.
(2 marks)

6 The writer makes us take Bruno's side by focusing on his thoughts and feelings. We never learn what the Lieutenant thinks and that means we can't be as sympathetic towards him.

The description of the 'ball of anger' exploding shows us this exchange is really affecting Bruno.

It suggests he has been trying to stop feeling angry for a long time but he has finally been pushed too far. However, he realises his limitations and his lack of courage: 'made him wish that he had the courage'. This also makes us side with him as it shows he is realistic and feels like he has no hope of standing up for himself.

The reference to 'Mother and Father', names which have been made into proper nouns to show these are the names by which Bruno thinks of them and refers to them, reminds us that Bruno is a young child. The fact he hasn't abbreviated these names suggests he is obedient and respectful towards his parents; characteristics which also make us take his side.

The language is very precise and careful, and we get the impression we are in Bruno's mind. When you follow a character's thought process you are more likely to side with them.
(5 marks)

pages 104–105

Purpose = to promote summer events in Woking
Audience = 7–16 year olds and their parents
Text type = magazine article

1

Activity	Details
drama workshop	Develop theatre skills, explore exciting scripts, meet others, final performance to friends and family
cinema crafts workshop	Make costumes and props, afternoon film
arts workshop	African drumming, Mexican crafts,
Craft Co. workshop	T-shirt painting, salt-dough modelling, card-making, pot-decorating
dance and poetry	Work with professional dancers, contribute your ideas, final performance

(2 marks, 1 from each column

2

Examples of language used	What it suggests
'a packed programme'	The alliteration makes it sound fun and exciting.
'a huge range of activities'	The adjective 'huge' emphasises the large amount of activities to choose from.
'chance to shine'	The verb 'shine' is positive and makes it sound like a brilliant opportunity.

(2 marks)

3 The article makes the opportunities seem exciting and attractive through the use of positive language, making it clear you can try new things, and by using bright colour and clear layout.

The activities are made to seem exciting and fun by language such as 'packed programme of activities' and 'get your creative juices really flowing'. The alliteration of the 'p' in 'packed programme' makes the phrase really bouncy and energetic, a bit like the activities they are trying to

promote. The lists of activities also make it sound like there's lots to do which is really good when you're a teenager as you can get bored easily.

It might seem scary to join in with a workshop if you don't know anyone, but they mention the fact you can make new friends – 'meeting other young people'. This makes it seem more attractive as it's always good to meet other people with the same interests as you.

The presentation is attractive. The picture is of young people acting, which helps to show the

sort of things you might do. Bold print is used for each activity and this helps the reader as they can scan through the article and not have to read the bits they are not interested in.
(5 marks)

pages 106–107

Purpose = to persuade the reader to join LeisureTime Plus
Audience = Ms Holroyd/adults concerned about health and fitness
Text type = letter

1 Join LeisureTime Plus
(1 mark)

4

Example of negative phrase	Why the language is used in this way
'crowded, sweaty gyms'	The negative adjectives make the gym sound horrible.
'sergeant-major fitness instructors with the bark of a bulldog'	The adjective 'sergeant-major' makes the fitness instructors sound strict and nasty. The 'bark of a bulldog' emphasises this impression.

(1 mark each)

5 For example:
  • Informal, colloquial phrase: 'a walk in the park'
  • Why it is used: it makes it sound like the writer of the letter is friendly and approachable. This colloquialism makes the whole letter seem informal and as if the writer knows how the reader will find exercise.
(2 marks)

6 This letter makes joining LeisureTime Plus seem a good idea by making exercise seem like a vital part of life and explaining the benefits it might have. It uses opinion disguised as fact, 'Everybody knows the need to live a healthy lifestyle', to make its ideas seem logical and believable.

The letter has a friendly, approachable tone: 'but we'll be with you all the way'. This makes the company seem friendly and approachable which means the reader is more likely to join it.

It uses emotive language and the benefits of exercise are shown: 'fitter, healthier and happier'. This list of three makes it sound balanced. It also seems balanced and considered because it admits that exercise used to be unpleasant: 'crowded, sweaty gyms and sergeant-major fitness instructors with the bark of a bulldog'. Juxtaposing this with what LeisureTime Plus offers makes its product seem even better. It also seems more truthful because it admits how bad exercise used to be.

Finally, by addressing the reader directly, 'you'll notice', it makes it more personal which is effective.
(5 marks)

2 Ms Holroyd seems like someone who is interested in keeping fit and healthy but has not found it easy. Perhaps she has had a bad experience of gyms and fitness instruction.
(2 marks)

3 *Any two of:*
  • The letter uses statistics to support its claims about the value of exercise.
  • It provides a list of benefits, suggesting there are lots of good results to be had from exercise.
  • It uses positive language to describe the benefits of exercise.
  • It uses 'experts' to support its claims.
(2 marks. Note, the question does not ask what the letter says, it asks about the methods used.)

pages 108–109

Purpose = to inform of the decision to give mobile phones to schoolkids
Audience = adults
Text type = newspaper

1 *Any two of:*
  • Personal organisers
  • Record lessons
  • Set alarm to remind to do homework
  • Use the memo
  • Research using the Internet
  • Share ideas in class
  • Manipulate sounds in music
  • Morning alarm
(1 mark for the two answers. 1/2 marks are not given.)

2 By the use of the connective 'However'. This tells us the information that follows will be different to the ideas that have already been presented.
(1 mark)

3 It suggests the world is modern and changing. The abbreviation 'techno' creates the impression of something fast-moving.
(1 mark)

4 Having a quotation from a named education advisor gives the story credibility and makes it seem more factual, despite the fact that he is just expressing an opinion.
(1 mark)

5 *Any two of the following. A total of two marks are available, one for each word or phrase selected with explanation.*
- 'claiming' suggests the teachers' view is just opinion and not correct
- 'constantly interrupting' makes the phones sound like a real ongoing nuisance
- 'demand' makes the teachers sound unreasonable
- 'dilapidated' emphasises the poor condition of the school buildings in an emotive way
(2 marks)

6 The views are not presented in a balanced manner. Firstly, the positive, government view is given more space and a quotation is included. Secondly, the teachers' views are presented with negative vocabulary and finally, the students aren't given a voice at all.

The mobile phone deal is presented in a positive way, with 'celebrating' by ministers and being described as 'a huge step forward'. These words and phrases create a positive impression of the deal and don't question it at all. Describing the world as 'techno' reminds the reader it is changing quickly and so learning must also change to keep up.

Wayne Daniels is presented as an expert and his views are presented as fact, giving the whole scheme credibility. The example of how students might use the phones to help organise themselves and make them do homework is a very positive view. Any potential negative outcomes are ignored totally. The phrase 'reel off lists of benefits' creates the impression that the benefits are so numerous that it's easy to list them.

The view of the teachers is presented very negatively after this innovation has been presented in such a positive way. We are told the teachers are 'claiming' and 'demand', words which sound very negative and aggressive. This tone makes us regard the teachers' view with suspicion.

Although the students are said to be 'celebrating', no student's view is reported so they aren't really given a voice. The use of the exclamation mark suggests that it's inevitable that students will celebrate and implies that the reporter didn't even go and interview them.
(5 marks)

pages 110–111

Purpose = to describe
Audience = teenage to adult
Text type = poem

1 The blackberries go mouldy and start to decay.
(1 mark)

2 It suggests they are desperate to collect all the blackberries so use any container they can get hold of.
(1 mark)

3 The final line, 'Each year I hoped they'd keep, knew they would not.' is balanced and shows that, although the narrator hopes they will keep, he knows they will rot. It gives the idea of a child clinging to hope when he or she knows deep down that time is passing and the natural world decays.
(1 mark)

4

Simile	Explanation
• 'hard as a knot'	This image describes how the unripe berries look and reminds us how hard and tightly formed they are. It also suggests they are dry and without their juice, as they are not yet ripe.
• 'like thickened wine'	This image makes the berry seem luscious and reminds us of its thick, potent juice.
• 'like a plate of eyes'	This is a horrible image and makes us think of the texture of the berries and the fact they have been stripped from the bush. They are shiny and reflecting all that is around them.
• 'palms sticky as Bluebeard's'	Bluebeard was a murderer, so this suggests the blackberry pickers are also murderers – they have picked all the berries, even though they know they won't keep.

(3 marks, one for a simile and two for its explanation)

5 The blackberry pickers seem eager, focused and hard-working. The speaker in the poem has a 'lust for picking', which suggests a desire you associate with a child rather then an adult. When the berries are ripe they use anything they can to collect them in, 'milk-cans, pea-tins, jam-pots', suggesting this is not an organised or professional harvesting. They don't mind the briars that scratch them as they are just focused on picking the berries.

The comment at the end, 'I always felt like crying' suggests the speaker was a child at the time of the blackberry picking, who hadn't yet learnt that the berries would rot and go off.
(5 marks)

6 The poet presents this memory as one that is good, but there is sadness mixed in with it. The excitement of the first 'glossy purple' blackberry creates 'lust', perhaps reflecting childish wonder at the natural world. However, there are many sinister images used in the poem which warn us that these wonderful berries are not the juicy treats they seem at first. We are told they are full of 'summer's blood' and there are other aspects of the natural world mentioned, such as the briars attacking them when they are picking the blackberries. This suggests they are robbing nature and shouldn't be taking so many berries.

By the end of the first stanza they have hands like 'Bluebeard's', likening them to a murderer. The sinister tone continues as we find the hoarded berries start to rot, 'rat-grey fungus, glutting on our cache'. Nature has won after all and although they have picked the berries they are not able to enjoy them all. Perhaps this is why there is a tone a sadness at the end of the poem. The adult poet looks back and realises it is not worth fighting nature. He is sad at his younger, naïve self, who will soon learn to stop hoping.
(5 marks)

pages 112–113

Purpose = to instruct the reader how to make a pizza
Audience = children/young people
Text type = recipe

1

Put the mozzarella on the pizza	2
Put your favourite toppings on the pizza	3
Make the tomato topping	1
Put the pizza in the oven	4

(1 mark)

2 This recipe is written for children or young cooks. I know this because of the language used such as 'fave' and 'scrummiest' and the way it suggests the reader gets an adult to help use the oven.
(3 marks)

3 *Any one of:*
- First
- Next
- Now
- When

These words are all connectives. They create a sense of order and logical progression. The reader knows not to move on to a new step before completing the previous one.
(3 marks)

4 *For example:*
- 'How to make the scrummiest pizza'
- 'our fave toppings'
- 'plaster it with the tomato topping'
You'll also need an explanation along the lines of this one:
Using the abbreviation 'fave' makes this recipe seem fun and the author seem friendly. It's aimed at young cooks and it makes the writer seem like someone who will enjoy the same sort of food. Pizza is also a fun food so this word fits it well.
(2 marks)

5 It says 'Sometimes simple is best' because cheese and tomato sounds really boring when you think of all the toppings you could have on a pizza. It acknowledges this fact but reminds the reader that this classic topping is actually really nice.
(2 marks)

6 I think this text will make young people want to make the pizza. It makes the recipe seem fun by its use of colour and bright layout. It also uses language to make cooking seem exciting, for example 'fave' and 'mouth-watering'. It makes it clear that you can make the pizza with any toppings you like, 'there are no rules', and this sounds really creative and fun.

The text makes a connection with the reader by addressing them directly with the pronoun 'you' and by using language that the young cook might use with their friends, 'scrummiest' and 'fave'. This makes the reader think that the pizza is going to be suitable for a young person to eat and won't be boring food like you normally get in recipe books.

It also makes the recipe seem easy by using words such as 'plaster', which suggests you don't have to be really careful with everything, and saying 'there are no rules', which is really appealing for a young cook!
(5 marks)

pages 114–117

Purpose = to entertain
Audience = adults
Text type = prose fiction

1 He was in prison because he murdered his brother-in-law but he has now escaped.
(1 mark)

2 The jailer is called Burton Duff. *(1 mark)*

3

Example of descriptive phrase	Impression it creates
'the moon sailed into a patch of unclouded sky'	The moon is free and moves easily. This contrasts with the actions of the fugitive.
'as white as death'	This simile suggests danger and evil and warns us that the figure pointing Orrin towards the jail might be a ghost.
'the livid mark of the iron bar'	The word 'livid' stands out just as the mark left by the iron bar. It is shocking and creates the impression of violence and danger.

(2 marks)

4a) The first sentence tells us that Orrin Brower comes from Kentucky, murdered his brother-in-law and has escaped from the law.
(1 mark)

b) It tells us lots of information very quickly to get us interested in the character and the story. It also means we know the background so the story can get going.
(1 mark)

5 *For example:*
'he saw, indistinctly, the figure of a man' or 'as white as death'.

You need an explanation such as:
The fact Orrin doesn't see his captor properly suggests something is strange about it. It doesn't speak to him, just points, and this is also unusual for someone capturing a wanted murderer.
(2 marks)

6 The author makes the ending of the story very dramatic through sentence lengths and repetition.

The penultimate paragraph is very detailed and this helps you to get a good picture of what is happening. The repetition of 'Straight' emphasises the fact that Orrin is not resisting arrest at all and is returning straight to jail. We are given lots of detail about him opening the door, 'laid his hand upon the knob of the heavy iron door', which slows the pace down and raises the tension and suspense. This is followed by two very short sentences, almost as if we are seeing the scene in real life and following Orrin's thought processes.

The final twist in the tale, that the person who captured Orrin and returned him to jail was the person he killed earlier in the story, is made even more shocking by putting it in a paragraph by itself. This makes it stand out more and so we spend more time reading it as it tells us Orrin was captured by a ghost.
(5 marks)

pages 118–119

Purpose = to review and entertain
Audience = anyone interested in film
Text type = review

1 *Be careful with this type of question! It wants to know more than that the film got 5 out of 5.*
The five stars show the reviewer likes the film and they make the reader want to know more about it. They are a quick and easy way for someone to find a review of a good film.
(1 mark)

2 *For example:*
- 'the poor long-suffering Gromit' which reminds us that Gromit is easy-going and bad things always happen to him.
- 'cheese-loving Wallace' which tells us more about Wallace and reminds us of his character traits.
(1 mark)

3 The repetition of 'big' builds up our anticipation and makes the film seem even better.
(2 marks)

4 *For example:*
Fact: it has been ten years since the last Wallace and Gromit film. *(Note you have to leave out the words 'long' and 'poor long-suffering' as these are opinions.)*

The reviewer starts the review with a fact embedded in opinion to make the whole review seem more factual. This will make us more likely to believe it.
(2 marks)

5 *For example:*
The phrase 'Maybe that means they weren't really needed?' is friendly and informal because it is as if the reviewer is just thinking aloud. This makes the reader think they are being very genuine and sincere, and we are reading their real thoughts.
(2 marks)

6 The positive language and tone of this review help to create the impression that this film is worth watching. Words such as 'Another' in the first line remind us that previous films have been fun to watch and suggest that if you enjoyed them you'd enjoy this one.

The use of exclamation marks creates a sense of excitement and this adds to the idea that the film is really good. Furthermore, words and phrases such as 'guaranteed to delight' are big

6

claims and make it clear the reviewer likes the film, even without the five stars.

The reviewer includes positive language such as 'joy' and 'energy' to make this a positive review. Mentioning Computer Generated Imagery provides us with contrast and something to measure this film against. Recent CGI films have been really impressive, and this comparison is suggesting this film is even better.

The final sentence is a paragraph on its own which makes it stand out more. Finishing with the reminder that it won an Oscar helps to promote the film in a positive way.
(5 marks)

pages 120–121

Purpose = to promote the school and invite prospective parents to an open day
Audience = prospective parents
Text type = formal letter

1 The head has written this letter to promote the school and to invite prospective parents to an open day.
(1 mark)

2 The head mentions Oxbridge twice. This suggests he regards students getting into those universities as his greatest successes. He doesn't mention other school-leavers. It also suggests this is what he thinks the parents are interested in.
(2 marks)

3 The head uses 'we' to show that he represents the whole school. It makes it seem as if he can speak for the whole school and that they are a united community. He wants to create the impression that the school is working well as a community and that they all get on and want the same things.
(2 marks)

4 This letter uses short paragraphs to help categorise the information and make it easier for the reader to understand. It also makes it more formal as it makes it seem as if it is all very organised and there is no room for change.
(1 mark)

6 Bordondown School is made to seem very organised and successful with the mention of 'examination results' and Oxbridge. By saying they are looking forward to '<u>Another</u> year' of top results it implies previous years have been really successful.

The school also seems very strict. It mentions learning three times but gives examples about uniform and homework showing that it thinks

these are important. The phrase 'we find an organised student is a successful student' is almost robotic and reminds me of the Demon Headmaster! The use of the word 'insist' shows there is no choice.

It mentions 'many' extra-curricular activities, but it doesn't list any, instead it suggests the parent 'browse' through the prospectus. The word 'browse' is one of the only informal words here, perhaps suggesting that the head doesn't really know what activities are available?

Overall, the impression the letter creates of the school is one of an organised and strict place with good exam results.
(5 marks)

pages 122–135

1 Staff look out for darker donations because these might have bacterial contamination or have been stored incorrectly.
(1 mark)

2 *Any two of:*
   • Donors will read it before they read the article and it will reassure them the process is safe.
   • Donors will read it before they read the article and it will interest them in the whole article.
   • It reassures potential donors that the process is safe.
   • It outlines another safety check that is undertaken.
   • It makes the staff seem like trained experts.
   • It includes lots of safety checks.
   (2 marks)

3 Describing the staff as 'scientific' increases our trust in them and makes them seem like professional experts who know what they are doing.
(1 mark)

4a The writer uses modal verbs such as 'can', 'could' and 'may' to show you cannot draw a direct conclusion from the colour of plasma.
   (2 marks – 1 for the term 'modal verb' and one for the use of examples. You do not need all three examples.)

4b *You might have one of the following ideas:*
   • The writer has done this to introduce ambiguity and show there are many possibilities.
   • It will ensure the reader does not jump to conclusions – it is too complex to do so.
   • It makes the whole process seem very complicated and the people who deal with it seem very skilled.
   (1 mark)

5 The subject matter is obviously going to be of interest to the audience as they are all blood donors. It has probably been included in this booklet to help explain what happens to the blood that is donated and to encourage people to keep being donors. It shows that the blood is really cared for and this implies how much it is needed.

The piece has been written in an informal but informative way. The facts give it authority and the rhetorical questions such as 'Have you been concerned your blood looks more like Ribena than the finest Merlot?' help to engage the reader in a fun and everyday way. The use of 'finest Merlot' when talking about blood also introduces a sense of humour. Although the language contains lots of technical terms such as 'haemoglobin', these do not make the piece off-putting as the rest uses everyday language.

The whole article is presented in an accessible way. The columns break the writing up and the eye is drawn to the pictures and information in boxes. Once you have read that you are more likely to read the whole article.
(5 marks)

6 Platelets help to clot blood. If your blood doesn't clot you won't stop bleeding when you get cut.
(1 mark)

7a The headings help to break the information up into chunks that are easy to read and learn.
(1 mark)

7b The bullet points help students to learn the information. This is a textbook, so the information needs to be very clear and obvious. Students don't have time to pick information out from long paragraphs.
(1 mark)

8a and b *You might have provided any of these answers:*
- (microbes) This gives a technical name for the organisms. Students can still understand the sentence even if they don't know the technical name.
- (blood proteins) These brackets provide more detail about the other chemicals in the blood.
- (slightly yellow) These brackets provide more detail about the 'almost colourless liquid'. The extra detail might help a student to remember it.
- (glucose, amino acids, fats) These brackets provide detail and specific examples of what the dissolved food is made up of.
- (carbon dioxide, urea) These brackets provide more detail about the waste products in plasma.
- (about 95 000 km) This provides the specific detail about the distance around the Earth.

(1 mark for the information in brackets and its explanation)

9 *You might have one of the following ideas:*
This text has been written to:
- help students to learn about blood.
- explain about blood.
- provide information about what blood is made up of.

(1 mark)

10 The extract makes the topic easy for the reader to follow by the use of layout and the general structure of the information. For example, sub-headings such as 'Red blood cells' and 'White blood cells' make it really clear what the paragraph is going to be about. This helps the reader to navigate as s/he can scan the text to find the section s/he needs. The pictures also help as they are really clear and link directly to the text – they illustrate it. Bullet points also help to break the text into easily manageable pieces.

The language is very technical because this is a technical subject. However, many technical terms are put into brackets so that the student can follow the text without them, or they are explained clearly, for example 'plasma'. On the whole the language is clear and simple, which means the reader is not going to be put off completely. Even if s/he doesn't understand the technical term it is likely they will be able to work it out. There are a lot of numbers in this extract, especially in the final paragraph. These give the piece credibility and make it seem more factual.

The piece is structured with many simple or compound sentences, mostly pretty short. This is because it needs to explain its knowledge quickly and clearly. It is not about revealing the interesting information with tension and suspense – it is about making it fast and clear.
(5 marks)

11 *You might have one of the following:*
- Watson thinks Holmes is clever. We know this because he asks how he knows about Afghanistan 'in astonishment'.
- Watson thinks Holmes is dedicated to his studies. We know this because he calls him a 'student … absorbed in his work'.
- Watson thinks Holmes gets very excited about things. We know this because he describes him as 'delighted as a child with a new toy'.

(2 marks: 1 for the idea and 1 for the quotation/evidence)

12 Holmes claims his idea is important because it will help apply justice and find out if a mark on the clothes of a suspect is blood or not.
(1 mark)

13 The writer has used alliteration of 'l' in 'lofty', 'lined' and 'littered' to make the room seem really big. The phrase 'lined and littered' emphasises the fact that it is full of scientific equipment. The sight seems almost overwhelming and this is supported by the word 'countless'.
(2 marks)

14 Sherlock Holmes is made to seem like someone fixated on an obsession in this extract. At first the whole room has been given over to his experiment; you can't even count the bottles of chemicals. Holmes is 'absorbed' and bent over the table – this makes him seem really obsessed.

However, when people enter the room he is excited and gives 'a cry of pleasure' which makes him seem more human. However, all he wants to do is show off his powers of deduction and the result of his experiment. This makes him seem quite selfish – he doesn't ask why they have come to visit, he just says, 'The question now is about haemoglobin'.

Finally, my impression is of someone who actually wants glory as well as justice as he names the test after himself – 'The Sherlock Holmes test'! He thinks he has made a great breakthrough for the world and is really pleased with himself. Overall, my impression is of someone who is self-interested and clever.
(5 marks)

Writing answers

pages 138–139

1

Text	Intended audience	Purpose
1	Local council members	Inform, describe, persuade
2	Your whole year group	Persuade, argue
3	Head teacher	Persuade, argue
4	Potential customer (head teacher)	Persuade, inform, explain
5	Project manager	Advise, review

2 **Level 7 (mid)**

Bridge School
Bridge Lane
Liverpool L13 7DG

Managing Director
Premium Cycle Sheds

Dear Sir,

Re: Cycle Sheds at Bridge School, Liverpool

It is with regret I have to complain about your product which was installed at my school last summer; they are simply not up to the job. As a consequence I wish to claim on the guarantee and have all the affected Sheds repaired or replaced immediately.

As a school we have made tremendous efforts to encourage students to take the healthy option and cycle to school; we hoped your product would be the finishing touch that helped them take this decision – we were providing them with state-of-the-art sheds to store their cycles away from the elements and potential thieves. This has not proved to be the case and the use of cycles has fallen dramatically as a consequence; that is very disappointing and frustrating.

I have tried to telephone you but have not been able to speak to you in person – I find this rather concerning and hope you will telephone me by return to discuss this issue and resolve it.

I look forward to hearing from you,

Tim Potter
Headteacher

This is level 7 because:

Sentence structure, punctuation and text organisation
- **Layout is correct** for a formal letter.
- **Full range of sentence structures** (simple, compound and complex) used for effect.
- **Ideas are developed and clarified.**
- **Connectives** such as 'as a consequence' have been used to signpost the train of thought to the reader.
- **Range of punctuation** to control and structure the letter.

Composition and effect
- **Tone matches task and audience.** The writer sounds authoritative.
- **Develops the ideas** to highlight the impact the problem has had on the school.

Spelling
- **Accurate, including complex, irregular words** such as 'immediately' and 'tremendous'.

3   Purpose = advise
    Audience = radio controller
    Text type = report

pages 140–141

1
negative	neutral	positive
dull	ordinary	stimulating
boring	normal	essential
tedious	necessary	exciting
mundane	commonplace	interesting
dull	usual	vital
wearisome		crucial
monotonous		

'Challenging' could be used in a positive or a negative way!

2   *There are lots of verbs available, for example:*
    a go: move, proceed, depart, journey, travel, advance
    b said: cried, shouted, mumbled, whispered, sobbed, pronounced
    c sleep: doze, slumber, nap, snooze, rest, drowse
    d cry: sob, wail, weep, bawl, howl, snivel
    e walk: stroll, saunter, plod, trudge, stride, march

3   *Here are some you might have thought of:*
    a This product is really *excellent / top class / first class / exceptional*.
    b I'll *talk to / call / meet* you later.
    c I *am not sure / don't know / am undecided* as to what to suggest.
    d *Hello / Good morning / Good evening / Good afternoon*.
    e We don't want to be *overcharged / given a bad deal*.

4   *Here are some possible similes:*
    a a really fierce deputy headteacher: as fierce as a bulldog
    b a jolly and cheerful football coach: like a beach ball on a sunny day
    c a huge grey factory: like a field of concrete
    d a small boat out at sea: as vulnerable as a butterfly
    e a child skiing down a mountain: like a fearless cannonball

5   *For example:*
    a Yob attacks grandmother.
    b The Guildford Flames slaughtered their opposition.
    c When the sun is blazing a cold drink tastes wonderful.
    d We are trapped inside the house by blankets of snow.
    e The ancient cat attempted to catch a bird and failed.

6   *For example:*
    a The man was attacked by the bear.
    b The woodland was damaged by a fire.
    c He quickly ate his burger.
    d She cried out as the young man took her handbag.
    e The old school buildings could be dangerous.

pages 142–143

1a I am very excited because I am going on holiday to America tomorrow! My whole family are going; what's really good is that I am allowed to take my best friend.

1b Cats are natural predators; when they see a bird or mouse it just means excitement to them. Sometimes they kill without the desire to eat their prey or can be shocked when they catch something.

2a The market was full of exciting smells, colours, noises, people and new things.

2b Music can create the atmosphere you need to learn; it can even help you to remember ideas. When you come to revise you can listen to the same music and it will help you to recall the original idea; your memory will have made a link.

3   *There are lots of possible answers. Here are some examples:*
    a At the end of the garden, beyond the tree, was the silent lake.
    b In the car, sitting quietly as directed, the boy watched the events unfold.
    c In the corner of the room, hidden by the shadows, crouched the murderer.

d Under the floorboards, in a dusty envelope, was the secret plan.

4 *In answers a–c, the main clauses are underlined and the subordinate clauses are in italics.*

   a <u>I hid under the duvet shaking</u>, *as the storm raged outside.*

   b <u>Claire</u>, *who was filled with a sense of relief,* <u>left the stage</u>.

   c *Until the power cut hit,* <u>Paul refused to leave his computer</u>.

Here are three possible answers for d–f:

   d Sally loved the book; she missed her bus because she was reading it.
   Sally, who missed a bus because she was reading, loved the book.
   Even though she missed her bus, Sally loved the book.

   e The computer finally died; it had been used non-stop.
   The computer, which had been used non-stop, finally died.
   Due to its non-stop use, the computer finally died.

   f Amanda bought some new pink shoes; she loved shopping.
   Amanda, who loved shopping, bought some new pink shoes.
   Loving shopping, Amanda bought some new pink shoes.

pages 144–145

1 When you first see my house you might think it's a bit dull and dingy because there are plants growing up the front wall and the path is a bit overgrown. I like to think this adds character and makes it more exciting when you come and visit me.

Stepping through the front door for the first time is normally a bit of a shock because we've painted the inside really bright colours. The woodwork (that's the doors and skirting boards) is pink and the walls are purple. My gran hates it, but we sat down and made a family decision so it's fine by us.

Once you are in you'll probably be drawn into the kitchen as there's generally something good cooking and that's where we tend to be. It's funny really, as it's the smallest room in the house but it's where we spend our time together. (Well, not the smallest, but you wouldn't all sit round the bathroom to talk about the day, would you?)

If I trust you, and the others say it's OK, I might take you to the end of the garden to see our den. It's taken us years to create it and it's simply the best place to be in the summer.

2 "Look, I'm really sorry," said Barry with frustration, "but this is just not going to work and that's an end to it." He threw down the play script and stood up to go.

Laura looked up at him, "I'm really sorry as well," she said with sarcasm, "I'm really sorry that we've wasted so much time rehearsing with you in the lead role when we could have had Lance. He would at least have listened to our ideas."

"That's just typical," replied Barry, "and that's why I'm leaving. You've never wanted me in this stupid play. Well, if you think Lance will have anything to do with you when he hears how you've treated me you've got another think coming!"

The rest of the cast sat watching with amazement as he coolly collected his jacket and walked out of the rehearsal room. Laura sat stunned.

"Did that really just happen?" she asked, "Did we finally get rid of that idiot?"

"Yes!" shouted Sian with joy, "Well done, you finally did it!"

3 *Firstly*, pre-heat the oven to 180°.
Secondly, take your vegetables and chop them into 1cm size cubes.
Then lightly oil the baking tray and arrange the vegetables on it so they are evenly spaced.
Next put the tray in the oven and set the timer to 40 minutes.
Finally remove the vegetables from the oven and enjoy!

pages 146–147

1 • Your address in the top right: *letter*
   • Impersonal phrases: *report*
   • The date: *letter, newspaper story*
   • Snappy headline: *newspaper story*
   • Alliteration: *letter, newspaper story, leaflet, speech*
   • Short paragraphs: *newspaper story, leaflet, report*
   • Bullet points: *leaflet, report*
   • Sign off of 'Yours faithfully, Yours sincerely' or a more informal phrase if you know the person: *letter*
   • Rhetorical techniques: *letter, newspaper story, leaflet, speech*
   • Entertain and inform: *letter, newspaper story, speech*
   • Informal style: *letter*
   • Repetition: *letter, newspaper story, leaflet, speech*
   • Clear but lively: *speech*
   • Factual: *report*
   • Formal address: *report*
   • Short sentences: *newspaper story, report*

- Clear statement of purpose: *report*
- Sub-heading: *newspaper story, leaflet*
- Modal verbs: *leaflet, report, speech*
- Emotive language: *letter, newspaper story, leaflet, speech*
- Personal pronouns: *letter, leaflet, speech*
- The address of the person you are writing to in the top left: *letter*

- Formal style: *letter, newspaper story, leaflet, report, speech*
- Quotations from experts: *newspaper story, speech*
- Pattern of three: *newspaper story, leaflet, speech*
- Varied length of sentences: *letter, leaflet, speech*

2

headline   *sub-heading*

PET FISH FRIED
Fish lover left red-faced

Paul Roberts, fish owning expert, was left red-faced yesterday, after he managed to fry hundreds of pounds worth of Koi Carp.

Roberts, who travels the world advising on the care of these creatures, fitted his own water filter system, something he advises his readers to leave to the professionals.

Unfortunately, he made a fatal error with the wiring and managed to heat his pond to near-tropical temperatures! The poor fish didn't stand a chance, as their home boiled and then exploded.

The stone pond exploded under the pressure of the boiling water and the boiled carp were sent flying. "My cat thought it was wonderful as cooked fish came flying through the air" explained Roberts' neighbour, Brian Downing, "although it was a horrendous noise!"

Roberts wasn't available for comment, but his wife said he was shocked and very saddened.

£400 Koi cat food

caption   *illustration*

3

alliteration

"Everybody knows that litter is <u>dirty and dangerous</u>. <u>So why do we just drop our litter?</u>

repetition

Rats are attracted to places with lots of litter, such as our school. Now, you might have an idea of <u>rats as <u>cute and cuddly, but they</u> actually spread <u>dangerous diseases</u> such as <u>cholera, typhus and leptospirosis</u>. We do not want these around our school, <u>so why do we just drop our litter?</u>

alliteration
list of three

<u>We need to make a stand. We need to make a difference. You need to make a difference.</u>

repetition/ list of three

Firstly, take responsibility for your own actions. Put your litter in a bin or your bag.

Secondly, take responsibility for our community. Challenge anyone you see dropping litter. Explain what the consequences could be and ask them to put their litter in a bin.

Finally, if you see a piece of litter, <u>don't walk over it: deal with it.</u> By doing this you will <u>make a difference</u>."

emotive language

repetition

pages 148–149

1 **a** I am going to the shop to buy some crisps and my dog needs to walk.

  b The shopping centre banned teenagers as they were bad news, they thought.

  c James and Amanda are going to France to learn to ski; I hope they enjoy it.

  d I can't believe Top of the Pops is still going after all these years; it's really amazing.

  e My English teacher is going to be really impressed with my improved writing skills.

2 **a** You will need a pen, a pencil and a ruler.

  b I had a great birthday, thanks.

    OR I had a great birthday – thanks.

  c Jane likes Shakespeare; Caroline prefers modern drama.

  d The bread (which was actually put out for the birds) had been eaten by the cat.

    OR The bread, which was actually put out for the birds, had been eaten by the cat.

    OR The bread – which was actually put out for the birds – had been eaten by the cat.

3 **a** I'm **b** it's **c** they're **d** you're **e** we're

4 **a** he is **b** let us **c** could have **d** can not
  e we have

5 **a** Lucy's cats were hungry.

  b Let's all go round to Wayne's flat for a party.

  c I won all the prizes at my school's sports day.

  d My town's provision for young people is inadequate.

  e My brother's car is a heap of junk.

pages 150–151

1 **a** buses **b** tries **c** potatoes **d** churches
  e children **f** sheep **g** foxes **h** cars
  i tomatoes **j** businesses **k** calves **l** rushes

2 **a** to run   running   ran
  b to stop   stopping   stopped
  c to drop   dropping   dropped
  d to decide   deciding   decided
  e to watch   watching   watched
  f to form   forming   formed
  g to admit   admitting   admitted
  h to prefer   preferring   preferred
  i to benefit   benefiting   benefited
  j to state   stating   stated
  k to fight   fighting   fought
  l to begin   beginning   began

3 **a** accommodation   **g** interesting
  b assessment   **h** marriage
  c audience   **i** people
  d business   **j** receive
  e embarrass   **k** secondary
  f explanation   **l** separate

  m sincerely   **o** tomorrow
  n surprise   **p** weird

4 **a** Lance and Susan are looking forward to *their* holiday.

  b "*Whose* homework is this?" asked the teacher. "It doesn't have a name!"

  c The old house was very creepy at night because it was so *quiet*.

  d "You may all go to lunch *except* Katie."

  e You need to explain the *effect* of the metaphor.

  f Oh, look! My pen is over *there*.

  g "*Who's* up for swimming?" asked Andrea.

  h I was *quite* pleased with my homework but the teacher didn't seem impressed.

  i I've got to go up in assembly to *accept* a prize on behalf of my tutor group.

page 152   Level 7 (mid)

Dear Alex,

Thanks for your email, it must get really boring stuck in hospital and you've made me feel bad about moaning about school – I'll try to be more positive about it.

I'm really pleased you're getting better and I can't wait for you to come out – I've been reading more with you away so it's funny you should ask me to recommend a book

The best book I've read for a long time is the first of a series, which means there are more should you enjoy this one, starring a teenage spy called Alex Rider. Alex is only our age but he ends up being recruited by MI5 to go undercover. He doesn't really want to, but they make him (I won't spoil it by telling you how!)

Anyway, he has loads of really exciting adventures and ends up crashing through a roof! It's such a good read; as soon as I finished it I went back to the school library to borrow the following book.

I really don't want to give the plot away, but I can give you a few more details to explain why these books are so good. Firstly, Alex is funny and normal – he really could be you or me! Secondly, each chapter contains something exciting which means you don't get bored. Finally, Alex has these really cool gadgets: a Gameboy which is also a bug decector, zit cream which dissolves metal and exploding chewing gum are just three of the wonderful things that have been invented for him

Interested yet? Go on, give it a go, you'll love it!

Sorry I don't have more time to write but I want to get back to my book!

See you soon,
Max

This is level 7 because:

Sentence structure, punctuation and text organisation
- **Full range of sentence structures** used to control the writing and create different effects.
- **Ideas are developed and clarified** – and, like Sebastian, Max provides evidence to support his ideas. However, he is better than Sebastian because he develops these ideas with more detail.
- **Controlled and fluent.** This email really flows well from the start to the finish. He has used a variety of techniques to do this such as the sentence structures, punctuation and connectives.
- **Use of connectives, summarising and generalising.** These also help the reader to follow the argument, especially, 'firstly', 'secondly' and 'finally'.
- **Range of punctuation** to clarify meaning and create particular effects. Max is very fond of the dash '–' and uses it to add ideas on. This is suitable in this piece of writing as it creates a sense of someone chatting informally to a friend, as he has been asked to do in this task.

Composition and effect
- **Tone matches task and audience.** The structure and vocabulary help to create an informal but informative tone – exactly what is required.
- **Thoughtful and supported.** Max has obviously planned his ideas before writing.
- **Developed and rounded.** The whole email provides the details and ideas asked for.

Spelling
- **Accurate,** including complex, irregular words. Max is a good speller and gets complex words such as 'recommend' and 'dissolves'. However, he isn't perfect – can you spot his error?

page 153 Level 7 (high)

Results of the uniform survey

The survey demonstrated a comprehensive desire to change the current old-fashioned and impractical school uniform. It was felt that the current uniform was uncomfortable and restricted movement in lessons such as drama, especially for girls who would like the opportunity to wear trousers.

As a consequence we advise a change of uniform.

In order to get full student approval the survey suggests an elected team of students should help to design three uniforms from which the students could then choose via a vote. The uniform should be practical and simple, not replicating today's fashions, but aiming to be timeless. Furthermore, KS4 students would like to wear something slightly different, perhaps a different coloured jacket, to distinguish them from the lower school.

We suggest the following:
1. Ask students what they want in a uniform.
2. Elect a student group to contribute to the decision-making team.
3. Produce three options.
4. The whole school votes for the best uniform.

This is level 7 because:

Sentence structure, punctuation and text organisation
- **Range of sentence structures,** including embedded subordinate clauses ('The uniform should be practical and simple, <u>not replicating today's fashions</u>, but aiming to be timeless.'). These make the writing sophisticated and allow the writer to add in little comments which add to the whole commentary.
- **Range of punctuation,** used accurately, to support meaning and help the piece to flow.
- **Good use of connectives** such as 'furthermore' and 'as a consequence' to give clarity and move the ideas on.

Composition and effect
- **Tone and structure match purpose and audience.**
- **Appropriate and thoughtful.** This commentary is balanced and provides real ideas and reasons for those ideas. This is exactly what is required.
- **Range of stylistic devices,** such as the numbered suggestions, help to make this a sophisticated piece of writing.

Spelling
- **Secure spelling,** including advanced vocabulary such as 'comprehensive' and 'distinguish'.

page 154 Level 7 (high)

My great-grandmother is a fascinating and inspiring lady, even if she is slightly scary at times.

She has amazing stories of her experiences in the war; she was a taxi-driver for the army and got to see things she shouldn't have seen and go places she shouldn't have gone. She tells you her stories, and you can imagine every tiny detail: her memory really is amazing.

One of my favourite stories is when she helped a group of soldiers get back to their base after dark, when they should have been back hours ago. She got some ladders, put them in her car and drove to the back wall of the base, reversing right up to the wall. Working together, they balanced the ladders on the car and managed to climb up and over! Then she dismantled them and drove away without lights so she couldn't be seen! Apparently the soldiers got away with it and they always made sure they had her as a driver after that!

The only problem with my great-grandmother is she gets really frustrated: she's been all over the world and done so many things but now she's stuck in a nursing home. I can understand her frustration but it really upsets my mum when we get home after visiting.

She's a great person though, and I'm proud to be related to her.

This is level 7 because:

Sentence structure, punctuation and text organisation
- **Range of sentence structures** used to develop the argument and clarify ideas.
- **Use of colons and semi-colons** is accurate and helps to structure and pace the description.
- **Paragraphs of different lengths.** This moves the writing on and creates impact (such as the last sentence being a paragraph by itself).

Composition and effect
- **Tone fits purpose and audience.** This is a formal piece about a personal subject so this can be difficult to do.
- **Individual viewpoint acknowledges other perspectives.** The comment about the great-grandmother being frustrated and the mother being upset shows understanding – this helps to create depth.
- **Appropriate and individual style** conveys thoughtful and balanced ideas.

Spelling
- Accurate.

page 155   Level 7 (low)

The holiday for us

I know we all like doing different things, that's why I think this is our ideal holiday.

There is something for each of us, and something different for every day for those of us who get bored quickly (that's you I'm thinking of, Tim).

For example, Tim, you like music and outdoor sports. This holiday offers both of these at a really exciting level. If the weather's good you can learn to windsurf or even dive; if bad you can stay in and improve your drumming. In fact, you might even meet your future super-star band members here!

Mum likes gardening and that's available too. She can learn more about plants and develop her skills; this will be great for all of us as it might stop her killing things when we return home!

And as for me? Well I don't really know where to start: can I try everything?

You see, it's the holiday for us. You know it is.

This is level 7 because:

Sentence structure, punctuation and text organisation
- **Range of sentence structures** used to develop the argument and clarify ideas. The use of add-in comments in brackets adds a sense of the personal, which is appropriate for this purpose and audience.
- **Expanded noun phrases**, such as 'your future super-star band members', add detail.
- **Range of devices** such as connectives give clarity and help the reader to follow the line of argument.

Composition and effect
- **Tone fits purpose and audience.** The direct address to Tim really helps here.
- **Individual viewpoint but sees the problems involved.** The response makes it clear that the family will all want something different and addresses those issues.
- **Appropriate and individual style** showing thoughtful and balanced ideas. The summary of the different options for each family member shows the writer has thought of each of them.

Spelling
- **Accurate.**

page 156   Level 7 (mid)

The air was finally silent.

Ann's body was finally still.

They had landed on Planet X; the first humans ever to get this far into space; the first humans to land on this planet. If all went to plan they would also be the first humans to walk on Planet X.

Ann forced herself to breathe. She turned to her team-mates hoping they wouldn't see how ridiculously excited she was.

"Ready?" she asked.

"Ready," came back the confirmation. Slightly nervous from Mark, she thought, but then, who wouldn't be.

"Ive done the final checks. It all looks good. We can move to Phase F." said Afsheen trying to disguise his desperation to get out there and explore. He knew the dangers. It was just he also knew of the adventure ahead. He was such an adrenalin junkie. Ann smiled to herself. She also wanted to get out there, get away from this spaceship after a whole painful year of being stuck inside it, drinking meals that tasted of chemicals and having to put up with these two!

She looked at the viewing screens again. It looked beautiful outside. Pink mists swirled around as if dancing, begging her to join them. The checks were clear; she would soon be out there.

"Come on Ann, get on with your tasks and stop daydreaming!" laughed Afsheen who was operating computer equipment as he spoke. She shook her head and did as he said.

Eventually, after all checks and double-checks and treble-checks were complete, they were ready. Ann and Afsheen lined up to go into the air lock. Ann turned to pat Mark on the back, "here goes!" she said.

With a hiss the first door opened. They stepped through.

The air lock drained and external air was sucked in.

Afsheen signalled to continue and the exterior doors opened. They stepped out into the beauty of Planet X.

This is level 7 because:

Sentence structure and punctuation
- **Wide range of sentence structures and paragraph lengths** manipulate the pace.
- **Narrative controlled in a sophisticated way.** The opening makes you think Ann is dead and then you realise she is in space – this is really clever as it involves the reader and makes the story exciting.
- **Wide range of punctuation**, such as the semi-colon.

Text structure and organisation
- **Shaped and controlled.** It starts and ends really cleverly, making you want to read more.
- **Cohesive and develops clearly.** The story is easy to follow and interesting.
- **Shaped and balanced.** The story is the chapter that is asked for – it opens and ends in a clever way and makes you want to read on.

Composition and effect
- **Controlled sequencing of narration with careful use of dialogue.** The student has obviously planned really carefully as it develops so well throughout the piece. Speech is used to add to the story and tell us more about the characters and events but it is not relied on to do the whole thing.
- **Viewpoint effectively sustained** throughout.
- **Well-chosen vocabulary and images.**

page 158 `Level 7 (mid)`

My Town – worth a visit?

Sleepy, pretty and just a little bit dull: that's my town for you! If you just drive through you'll be left with an impression of chocolate-box houses and gardens, which is fair enough: the houses and gardens are pretty. It's just that pretty doesn't always make somewhere a good place to live.

The beautiful setting is matched by a sleepy atmosphere, at least, sleepy on the surface. When you've lived here for a few years (as I have), you'll realise it's actually full of really bored teenagers who simply have nothing to do in the evenings if they can't nag a parent or older sibling into driving them out of the place.

Local Life – what's going on

As you will have guessed from what I've already written, there's not much going on if you can't get out of the place. The cinema, sports centre, ice-rink and youth club are all in the next town – 7 miles away! There are shops, I'll give you that, but what teenager wants to shop in the Ye Olde Corner Shoppe more than once a week (and that's if they let you in, but I won't go there).

If you are an old person this must be a great place. You can wander around and drink tea with your friends day after day. If you've got a car, this must be a great place: you can get out. If you are a kid, this must be a great place: you can meet your friends at the primary school. It's just once you hit secondary school age it all goes horribly wrong. Just imagine: I actually look forward to coming to school just so I can see my mates and do something!!! Surely that's unhealthy for a thirteen year-old boy??!

The best bits

Well, these obviously depend on the sort of person you are, but here's mine:
- The school bus – it's generally late but it provides a good opportunity to gossip about what happened at school the day before.
- The Ye Olde Corner Shoppe – let's face it, they do a good range of sours.
- The tree in my garden – ok, so I'm stretching it a bit. But it is a good tree. The best!

And that's about it. Sorry.

Things that need to be changed

This is a difficult one. OK, so the place is hopeless for teenagers, but there are only 7 of us. Maybe we just need a regular bus route? Or enough money for taxis out of here (dream on). My mum loves it here and is always going on about the fresh air and peaceful surroundings. She wouldn't change a thing.

Overall

Well, overall I reckon this is a good place to live if you can get out when you need to. Without transport you'll go mad!

This is level 7 because:

Sentence structure and punctuation
- **Wide range of sentence structures.** There are simple, compound and complex sentences, all used to lead the reader and control the pace and tone.

- **Ideas controlled** and in a sophisticated way. The writer takes you with him to the conclusion and manages to give you a real sense of his village.
- **Wide range of punctuation** used to enhance meaning and create particular effects. The pattern of three complex sentences, 'If you … , this must be a great place …' is a sophisticated technique that is used to very good effect.

Text structure and organisation

- **Shaped and controlled.** The whole piece really takes you through the experience of living in this village as a teenager. By the end you are really on the side of the writer.
- **Cohesive and develops clearly.** This is obviously planned as it develops confidently towards a shaped ending. Every part of it contributes to the whole.

Composition and effect

- **Attractive voice, clear and engaging.** This piece is enjoyable to read.
- **Viewpoint effectively sustained throughout.** Although there is one viewpoint promoted, it does show an awareness and understanding of other responses to the village.
- **Well-chosen examples and ideas.**

page 160   Level 7 (high)

Dear Great Uncle Quentin

Thank you for your letter, it was really interesting to read of your school days – I can't believe you were such a rebel!!! Mine are really boring in comparison, but the biggest thing that's happened recently has been option choices.

When we get to the end of Year 9 (as I am now), we are allowed to drop some subjects and start specialising; it's a bit of a scary prospect, actually, as it means I've got to start thinking of a career!!! Anyway, I've just made my option choices and so I thought I'd tell you what I've chosen.

Firstly, I have to keep the core subjects – this means English, maths, science and a language. This is fine by me because they are all going to be really useful and are exams you have to have for university and the future. They are all interesting and taught by good teachers so I should be fine, although I'm told you get loads of English homework in KS4.

So what have I chosen? Well, I've tried to pick a mix that will give me a balance but also things that I find interesting (there's no point doing something you can't stand). My first choice was geography. I chose this because it's fairly interesting and the teacher's crazy (in a good way!) We have to work hard, but when we've done the work she writes competitions and challenges for us to do. I really hope I get her next year.

My second choice was electronics. I really wanted to try something new and this fits with my interest in physics and maths. I'm not sure where it'll lead me, but I'll have a fun 2 years, inventing new things – you never know, I might invent an amazing new product and be a millionaire by the time I come to sit my GCSEs! (or not!!!)

Finally, I've chosen digital photography which is my 'fun' choice. I'm really looking forward to this one as the module I did of it earlier this year was brilliant and the work that the students have produced is really professional looking. Dad was a little worried this was going to be a waste of a GCSE choice, but with all the others I've got to do I persuaded him I needed a 'fun' choice – let's hope it's as good as I think it'll be.

Right, hope that's all clear. I'll hopefully be able to bring some of my photos when we next come and visit and then we'll see if I've wasted my options or not!

Looking forward to seeing you in the summer,

Lots of love,
Georgie

This is level 7 because:

Sentence structure and punctuation

- **Wide range of sentence structures.** The complex sentences, such as the first sentence of paragraph 2, offer lots of ideas but the punctuation is used to guide the reader through carefully. Putting information in brackets lets us know it is extra and is appropriate for a letter to a relative. Exclamation marks would also be avoided if it were for any other sort of audience.
- **Ideas controlled** and in a sophisticated way. The piece is obviously planned as it develops naturally and is clear to follow.
- **Wide range of punctuation.** The informal asides work really well here but it can be difficult to make this work.

Text structure and organisation

- **Shaped and controlled** to engage and guide the reader through it. Starter phrases such as 'So what have I chosen?' signal what is likely to come next and help us to receive the information.
- **Cohesive and well developed.** Everything in this piece contributes to the meaning of the whole.
- **Shaped and balanced.** Georgie rounds the letter off by mentioning a future meeting rather than just stopping suddenly. It also sets up a future conversation – a very sophisticated and mature thing to do!

Composition and effect

- **Attractive voice, clear and engaging.**

- **Viewpoint well sustained.** Georgie doesn't change her mind about any of the topics she writes about. This shows she has planned before starting to write.
- **Well-chosen examples and ideas.** Examples always help ideas to come to life.

page 162 Level 7 (high)

<u>MusicWrap: the new best way to listen to your music?</u>

What a great concept: I was looking forward to this test and review from the moment I heard about it. A music player, disguised as a watch, with wireless headphones: what could go wrong? Unfortunately, quite a lot.

The box arrived and I ripped open the cellophane wrapping, just as we all do in real life (it's an essential part of a new toy, really!). Running my hand over the pristine box I savoured my colleagues' jealousy; it had been a real battle to get this assignment. I opened the box, pulled out the shaped cardboard tray and …

I was greeted by a chunky, plastic, 80s watch. Something I wouldn't normally be seen dead wearing.

With laughter pealing around I defiantly put the watch on. And then I put it on again, higher up my arm so it would be hidden by my sleeve.

I started following the very complicated instructions regarding downloading my MP3s but then gave up and called the helpline. I'm reviewing their product: I'll get the best help.

At least that's what I thought. It didn't happen. After 2 hours and 12 minutes (my phone's got a call timer) I went back to the instructions. Then I threw it open to everyone in the office.

Now, we're a bunch of gadget-geeks. We love gadgets. We live for then, love them, dream of them. We couldn't get it to work.

And at this stage I gave up.

The product is too ugly to wear out, we can't figure out how to use it and the support line is just a money-eating 'please hold, we value your custom' affair. It's a pity as I was ready to make this the product of the decade: I wanted to make it the product of the decade. But I can't, and I can't even recommend it to you either. Sorry about that, but that's bad design for you.

Now where's my iPod…?

This is level 7 because:

Sentence structure and punctuation
- **Wide range of sentence structures.** These bring the review to life as they control the pace of the piece.

- **Ideas controlled** and in a sophisticated way. The overall structure is clearly planned and shaped to entertain as well as review.
- **Wide range of punctuation.** The use of direct comment to the reader really helps to connect with the reader.

Text structure and organisation
- **Shaped and controlled** to engage and guide the reader. Structures such as the patterns of three and the building phrases such as 'It's a pity as I was ready to make this the product of the decade: I wanted to make this the product of the decade' show the relationship between the product and the final opinion as expressed by the reviewer.
- **Cohesive and develops clearly.** It flows easily and the reader can see how the writer was disappointed by the product – making the bad review seem even worse.

Composition and effect
- **Attractive voice, clear and engaging.** The piece reads very personally – it is as if the reviewer is talking directly to the reader. This works well for a review as we need to trust the person reviewing the product. However, the reviewer is careful to maintain authority by mentioning the number of products s/he reviews so this doesn't just become a personal rant.
- **Viewpoint effectively sustained throughout.**
- **Well-chosen examples and ideas.**

page 164 Level 7 (mid)

Dear Mr Taylor (Planning Officer),

I wish to register my objection to the planning application made by Foods'R'us to build a new store where the skatepark currently is. My objection to this application is based on knowledge of what the local community needs and wants.

Firstly, there is the loss of the skatepark to consider. This was built with funds raised after a lengthy campaign by local families; to wipe it out would be a massive insult to them and make their time and effort worthless. This would not be a popular or good move.

Secondly, the skatepark is an essential aspect of life for this town. It provides local teenagers with a safe and secure place to meet; as well as keeping them out of everyone else's way. I know some people think we are a threat, all hanging together at the park, but just come and talk to us and you will see we are not.

In addition, without the skatepark there will be nothing for us to do, as well as nowhere to go, and bored teenagers could lead to trouble in the town.

Next we must consider the need of the local community for another supermarket. Considering we already have three large businesses of this sort, I am at a loss to understand why another is needed. Currently the town gets on really well, with small, local businesses balancing the huge multinational. If this balance is changed it will change the whole nature of the town as local shops will have to close down and local people will lose their livelihoods. Who could want that?

In conclusion, I ask you to reject the planning application and think of the needs of the town before the needs of the anonymous supermarket giant.

Thank you for your time,

Andrea Plumtree

This is level 7 because:

Sentence structure and punctuation
- **Wide range of sentence structures.** Complex sentences allow lots of ideas to be presented, and the relationship between them indicated.
- **Ideas controlled** and in a sophisticated way. The paragraphs build the ideas up gradually and in layers – this helps to add strength to the whole piece.
- **Wide range of punctuation** used to enhance meaning and connect with the reader.

Text structure and organisation
- **Shaped and controlled** to engage and guide the reader. This must have been planned carefully as it builds up so carefully and concludes with real strength from the careful argument.
- **Cohesive and develops clearly.** All the small ideas fit together and add to the whole letter.

Composition and effect
- **Attractive voice**, clear and engaging. Although this letter is promoting one point of view it does not appear aggressive, which can be off-putting. It appears to be a considered and logical point of view.
- **Viewpoint effectively sustained throughout.** The use of evidence and detail helps this.
- **Good use of rhetorical devices**, such as the rhetorical question and pattern of three.

page 168   Level 7 (high)

Dear Chair of Governors,

I have just heard of the generous gift by Liz Day and am pleased to be able to offer some ideas as to how to spend this money.

Everybody knows that exercise is vital for a healthy life, whether a child or an adult. However, did you know that students today spend more time sitting still behind desks than ever before? These two facts are compelling reasons to spend the money on developing our sports provision.

Experts have conducted many research projects that show 20 minutes exercise every day helps learning as well as developing health and strength. If, as a school, we provide this opportunity for our students, we will not only be helping them grow, but also to learn. How can we ignore this opportunity?

The obvious way to spend this generous gift is on our sports provision; this will make a significant difference to the lives of our students and staff, and the money is for the whole school. If we build a swimming pool we will also be able to ensure every member of our school community has the vital life skill of swimming. We will also be able to hire the pool out in evenings and at weekends and make loads of money for the school; all round this is a fabulous opportunity.

I hope you will take these ideas on board and investigate them fully. I would be happy to help wherever possible.

Thank you for your time; it's good to know we students have a voice.

Yours faithfully
Sue Jones

This is level 7 because:

Sentence structure and punctuation
- **Wide range of sentence structures**, including complex sentences, used skilfully.
- **Ideas controlled** and in a sophisticated way. The letter involves and manipulates the reader, making the suggestions appear to be the only logical way to proceed.
- **Wide range of punctuation** enhances meaning and connects with the reader.
- **Rhetorical questions used to good effect**, as is the final complex sentence.

Text structure and organisation
- **Shaped and controlled** to engage and guide the reader. This letter has obviously been planned carefully as it develops each idea fully, with appropriate detail, and builds up to a convincing conclusion.
- **Cohesive and develops clearly.**
- **Shaped and balanced.**

Composition and effect
- **Attractive voice**, clear and engaging. The ideas are conveyed strongly, but the piece is not aggressive.

- **Viewpoint effectively sustained throughout.** The piece is focused and all the examples and ideas are used to drive it forward.
- **Good use of rhetorical devices**, especially rhetorical questions.

page 170 `Level 7 (mid)`

Teenage TV – the new top show

This exciting project could revolutionise TV today. Teenagers need programmes made for them that don't patronise them or bore them to death. My analysis of the research results suggests the following will be a winner:

Teen TV: A show that engages and excites teenagers across the country

- The magazine-style show is popular; we should aim for a teenage-style Richard and Judy – maybe we can get Ant and Dec?

- Live music from the top bands, and interviews where they talk about making music.

- Decent competitions means viewers will engage with the programme – we need to find a sponsor so we can have substantial prizes (mobile phone? iPod? adventure holidays?).

- Each item must be fast-paced and have a link to the audience – not whoever wants to promote their book/new show/film.

- It must be professional and slick; this audience knows when it's being patronised.

- Dating and relationship tips: maybe include some psychology/relationship advice?

- Fashion – cutting edge, real fashions – not just baseball caps and hoodies!

Key tasks will be balancing the content to match the audience age and gender range.

The most important thing is finding the right presenters.

This is level 7 because:

Sentence structure, punctuation and text organisation
- **Full range of sentence structures**, including complex sentences. The bullet points are also a good way of organising this type of task.
- **Ideas developed and clarified** through the answer. They show real thought about the task and the ideas are explained clearly.
- **Range of punctuation**, such as the bullet points and sub-headings, used to clarify meaning and create particular effects.

Composition and effect
- **Tone matches task and audience.** The student sounds authoritative without being aggressive. It reads as if it's written by an expert who really knows his/her stuff.
- **Imagines and explores ideas fully.** There are lots of ideas provided and the answer covers a wide range of issues, all of which are relevant to the task.
- **A developed and rounded answer**, which must have been carefully planned as it develops so naturally.

Spelling
- **Accurate**, including complex irregular words such as 'substantial' and 'psychology'.

Shakespeare answers

The Tempest
page 176

1 1C, 2D, 3A, 4B

2

Quotation	Technique	Effect
'the wild waves whist'	alliteration of 'w'	Reflects the movement of the waves and spray
'the fringèd curtains of thine eye'	Metaphor – her eyelids are curtains and the lashes a fringe to the curtains	Reminds us that Prospero can send Miranda to sleep at will due to his magic and her eyes are key to her understanding the world. This metaphor now also has a modern meaning as theatres often have curtains that raise for the action
'thou shalt be as free As mountain winds'	Simile comparing freedom with how the mountain winds move	We remember that the mountain winds can go anywhere and everywhere and cannot be controlled – this is the freedom Ariel longs for
'But you – o you, So perfect and so peerless – are created Of every creature's best'	Alliteration of 'p' and 'c'	The repeated sounds link the words together and build up their strength

pages 178–179

What impression do you get of Miranda in these scenes?

> Level 6 (mid)

My impression of Miranda changes during these scenes; she seems to be the manipulated girl who finally thinks for herself and goes against her father's commands, but when you look at it again you have to question to what extent she is actually thinking for herself.

In the first scene (Act 1, scene 2), she is just her father's puppet – he even tells her where to look: 'the fringed curtains of thine eye advance'. Prospero describes Ferdinand to Miranda in really positive terms so she is more likely to fall in love with him. Prospero uses words like 'gallant', which suggests he's noble, which was a really good thing to be in those times. He also says he's 'stained with grief' so Miranda might feel more compassionate towards him and that this grief has been a cancer or 'canker' to his good looks – so Miranda will see that Ferdinand would normally look more handsome and this will also make her fall in love with him. It does the trick because she calls him 'A thing divine' and 'noble' which is really positive. Therefore my first impression of Miranda in these scenes is just like in the rest of the play where she is manipulated and controlled by her father. This has been going on for all her life so she doesn't even notice it.

When I first read the play I thought she changed and became stronger as she stood up to her father, but really she just behaves as he manipulates her into behaving, so my impressions of her have changed as I have read and re-read the play. Prospero does this really deliberately, 'I must uneasy make, lest too light winning Make the prize light'. The alliteration of the 'l's here links the key words together and makes them bounce, as if they are light and might fly away.

Although Miranda begs her father not to be horrid to Ferdinand she does obey his commands, maybe as she knows the power of his magic. My impressions of her here were originally of a girl who was really in instant love, but now I just see a girl who is totally controlled. She mutters about 'I have no ambition to see a goodlier man' but she doesn't really put up much of a fight. I also wonder about this instant 'love' as what will happen when she sees other men? Prospero does make a fair point.

21

And Ferdinand thought he was about to die, so can you also believe in his love? I'm not sure.

In the second set scene (Act 3, scene 1) Miranda seems to be speaking her own mind much more and going behind her father's back, 'my father is hard at study' but she's just following the course Prospero has planned for her, so it's hardly standing up for herself. She offers to carry the logs and says 'it would become me as well as it does you', and this reminds us that she is as noble, if not more noble, as Ferdinand, so they are a perfect match in those terms.

The time I have a really good impression of Miranda is when she doesn't understand the social conventions and tells Ferdinand she is a virgin and she wants to marry him. This just wouldn't have been done in those days but I really like it – it is the first time she is being herself and so my impression of her goes up.

This is level 6 because:

- It has a clear focus on the question and provides reference to it throughout the answer.

- It shows a clear and personal understanding and response to the characters.

- It uses references clearly to support and illustrate the answer.

- It shows that you can refine and change your ideas about the play as you study it.

To raise the level the student needs to:

- Keep the focus on Miranda and ensure all the points are made relevant to her character

- Include more analysis of the language, especially the effects of specific words and phrases.

- Develop the use of quotations so they are selected to illustrate an idea precisely.

What impression do you get of Ferdinand in these scenes?

Level 6 (high)

Ferdinand is really just a character whose function is to show Prospero's power and make his plans for a 'happy ending' possible. As a character, we are made to feel a bit sorry for him because of the situation he is in, but at the end of the day he's just someone who is sad and then in love.

When we first see Ferdinand he speaks beautifully about the sounds he can hear and his confusion. Lines such as 'this music crept by me' reminds us of the way the sounds and music of the island are almost alive – the verb 'crept' makes it quite sinister and he says it has 'drawn' him, once again personifying it with the ability to control him. This

reminds us of the power of Prospero and Ariel's magic and we realise that Ferdinand is now in the power of Prospero. We wonder why he is wanted and why he has been saved.

Ferdinand's instant attraction for Miranda might be seen as a result of his confusion – he thinks she's the 'goddess on whom these airs attend' and might be in awe or scared of her sudden appearance on this apparently deserted island at first. However, as he speaks to her he asks if she is 'maid or no', to see if she is human or divine. However, we know this also has a double meaning of 'are you a virgin or not?' which reminds us of the cultural context in which the play was written (or the official one anyway).

When Ferdinand is telling us that he is 'the best of them that speak this speech' we are reminded that he thinks his father etc is dead and we feel sorry for him again. At this point we get the impression of someone who knows his duty is to now step into his father's shoes and become king. He refers to himself as 'Naples' and this use of metaphor has a lot of power as it shows the responsibility he feels. The impression we get of him here is of someone who can deal with bad things and shocks and has always known that when his father does die he just has to step into the role rather than be full of grief.

The sudden attraction Ferdinand feels for Miranda is, just like hers for him, all based on appearance. He proposes to her really quickly (as long as she's a virgin!) so we have some sympathy with Prospero trying to calm things down a bit. We see Ferdinand here as someone who has just been through a lot and is overwhelmed with the woman he sees so unexpectedly.

In the second scene it is much the same. He is happy to move logs as it's for Miranda and he says he's fancied lots of women but she is the one he loves. We get the impression of someone who sees her as an escape – he did say that a glimpse of her would be like freedom from his prison. He uses really horrible language to say what this log moving task would normally be like to him: 'the flesh-fly blow my mouth'. The alliterated 'f' is like trying to blow a horrible fly off your face, but this fly is one that lays eggs in dead flesh and so is disgusting. We see the strength of his emotions and the way he is prepared to change his expectations for Miranda. We get the impression that he really loves her.

This is level 6 because:

- It has a clear focus on the question and provides reference to it throughout the answer.

- It provides quotations to support the ideas, and it provides explanation and analysis of these quotations.

- It provides detailed consideration of the language and how it affects the meaning.

To raise the level the student needs to:

- Plan the answer more carefully to ensure it is balanced and has enough on the second scene.

- Provide a conclusion that draws together all the key points.

page 180

How is the theme of love explored in these scenes?

Level 6 (mid)

These scenes show us different types of love: romantic love (between Miranda and Ferdinand) and filial love (the love of a child for a parent – this is Ferdinand for his father and Miranda for Prospero). In both cases the filial love is coming to an end, or changing as the children (Miranda and Ferdinand) experience romantic love.

Ferdinand's love for his father seems a bit subdued (you'd expect him to be really upset that his father might be dead) but he is really confused, especially due to the music that has 'drawn me' around the island to this place. We get the impression that he has grown up knowing that he can't have loads of emotions when his father dies because he will then be king and has to act like a king. He calls himself 'Naples' showing this formal side and we wonder if he is showing his love for his father by behaving in this way (because he is being really strong and acting like a king rather than crying all the time).

Miranda's love for her father is changed in this scene (as she meets Ferdinand). The moment she sees Ferdinand she calls him a 'thing divine' showing she thinks he's god-like (which links to him thinking she is a goddess – interesting that they use the same sort of language). Prospero doesn't want the two of them to undervalue their love because it was so easy and turns nasty and this causes Miranda to protest at the way he is treating her new love. This is where the love that Miranda has for her father changes as she can see he is being unreasonable and so she starts to question him (which she hasn't done before).

The love that Ferdinand and Miranda feel for each other is romantic love (as shown by them calling each other 'divine' and 'goddess') although it is totally based on appearances (so Prospero is probably right). They develop this love in the second set scene (where Ferdinand is carrying logs) and we keep on being told they are a good match for each other as they are both noble and still love each other. Ferdinand wouldn't normally do this

task but says it's not a problem as Miranda is there (either crying or talking to him). Ferdinand says she's precious and won't let her help and she goes against her father and tells Ferdinand her name. This romantic love is everything of dreams as he says she's 'so perfect and so peerless' (alliteration) and says he loves her more than anything in the world. As she feels the same they agree to get married and it looks like happily ever after and they soon go off to play chess.

The theme of love shows that love can be different sorts and can change (and should change as you grow up).

This is level 6 because

- It has a clear focus on the question and has structured the answer in a logical fashion.

- It shows a clear understanding of different types of love and makes good links between the characters.

- It shows excellent knowledge of the play.

To raise the level the student needs to:

- Provide more quotations as evidence and analyse what they tell us of the play.

- Provide analysis of language and its impact on our understanding and response.

- Avoid using brackets – the information is either needed or not.

page 182

The language used in these scenes emphasises the high emotions experienced by the characters. Explain how Shakespeare has used the language to create this emotion.

Level 6 (high)

The scene, and perhaps Ferdinand's emotions of confusion, is set by Ariel's songs full of alliteration, perfect rhyme and metaphor. The alliteration combines with the rhyme to create texture and atmosphere and the metaphor 'those are pearls that were his eyes' combines beauty and horror which is quite fitting for the high emotions Ferdinand is about to experience: he is going to go from thinking he is alone, his father is dead and all he knows is gone, to seeing the woman he will fall in love with. His life is about to change.

Ferdinand's own language takes its lead from Ariel with the alliteration which continues the texture and makes his words full of emotion. When he sees Miranda his language becomes more expansive, calling her a 'goddess' and 'you wonder', raising her to more than human, as his question 'if you be maid or no' suggests. This might seem a bit extreme but it reflects his high emotions and the way his life is changing from moment to moment.

Miranda's language matches Ferdinand's in that she calls him 'a thing divine'. The fact they both refer to each other as being godly or more than human shows the impact each has on the other. This tells us about the level of the emotion they are experiencing and how they are a good match as they are thinking in the same way and using the same sort of language.

Prospero's language is really harsh and he is really harsh with Miranda calling her 'wench' and when she objects to his treatment of Ferdinand calls her 'my foot my traitor' saying that she is only like his foot, something he steps on. He also calls her an infected worm which really does make it seem like he doesn't value her as a real person.

Miranda and Ferdinand's language in the second set scene is really similar to show that they are a perfect match. Ferdinand uses the metaphor of the blow-fly which is really horrible and makes us cringe. He also uses lots of alliteration such as 'perfect and peerless' which makes it link together and push forwards so it has lots of emphasis. Miranda's alliteration is the same, 'bigger bulk', it links and stands out – it becomes the bigger bulk she is talking about.

This is level 6 because:

- It provides clear explanation and analysis of the use of language in the set scenes.

- It makes links between the language of the different characters and shows how this has further meaning.

- It starts with a clear focus on the question.

To raise the level the student needs to:

- Keep referring to the actual question throughout the answer – this just becomes general analysis of the language. It is good but needs to be made relevant to the idea of high emotions.

- Write a proper conclusion – this answer just stops.

pages 184–185

Ferdinand's emotions change dramatically in this play. Imagine you are directing this play. Explain how you want the actor playing Ferdinand to show his thoughts and emotions in these scenes.

Level 7 (mid)

Ferdinand must be a difficult character to act as he really only functions to wrap up the loose ends of what to do with Miranda and set up the resolution and the future. These two scenes are his biggest but they are not terribly exciting although they cover a real range of emotions; when we meet him he is confused and mourning the supposed death of his father and everyone he knows but by the end of the second scene he is totally in love and looking to a future with Miranda.

The actor playing Ferdinand needs to get the combination of terror, sorrow and duty in the first part of Act 1, scene 2. Terror for being alone in this strange place, sorrow for the death of his father and all who accompanied them and duty as he now must be king and take the role he has been prepared for his whole life. The strangeness of the place is established with Ariel's song and continued with Ferdinand's description of the way the music 'crept by me' and 'drawn me'. These verbs personify the music, giving it the human qualities of persuasion and influence. Ferdinand needs to show his confusion and awareness of what has happened to him – he knows what the music has done so he is not as stupid as many of the people who end up on the island, he just doesn't understand how.

The first major point of change for Ferdinand is when he sees Miranda and we are shown this through his language, and so the actor must show that he is jolted into a different way of thinking and understanding as he sees this 'goddess'. It is interesting that both Miranda and Ferdinand see each other as god-like and that their language fits in this way – it shows us that they are suited. This was a common technique for Shakespeare; he often used level of language to show status and type of character and you could see if a couple were suited by their language.

We see Ferdinand's understanding of his duty when he identifies himself as 'Myself am Naples', this use of metonymy gives him the status of monarch and reminds us of the important role he plays for his people. The actor needs to be solemn as this is really serious: Ferdinand has lost a father, the country has lost a king, and the heir is missing. This must be a real time of confusion and turmoil for Ferdinand and the actor needs to show this.

Life is to get more confusing for Ferdinand as Prospero suddenly accuses him of being a spy and uses his magic on him again before making him move the logs. When we join Ferdinand in Act 3, scene 1 he is exhausted, confused but somehow jubilant as the thought of Miranda sustains him – 'the mistress which I serve quickens what's dead, and makes my labours pleasures'. Through the opening of this scene, and his conversation with Miranda, we see him make much use of alliteration and references to his nobility to create real contrast with his position and his task. Some of his language is incredibly descriptive, such as the flesh-fly comparison that really is stomach-turning. We see his personality though these words and realise that he is noble and a suitable partner for Miranda.

When Miranda and Ferdinand declare their love for each other the actor needs the lightest touch so this part of the scene doesn't become embarrassing. This love has been so instant and so based on appearance it is natural to be sceptical so it's the task of the actors to keep it real. The use of the 'h's through his last few lines help to keep it light, which will help.

By the end of the scene the Ferdinand we see is jubilant and exhilarated at his new love and future, his declaration, 'A thousand thousand!' needs to sum up his new lust for life so we see he is the opposite of where he was when we first met him.

This is level 7 because:

- It has a detailed understanding of the character and the language he uses.

- It provides clear and detailed analysis of the character and how and why he is behaving as he is.

- It has a clear focus on the question and keeps the answer focused on it throughout.

To raise the level the student needs to:

- Provide more short quotations rather than just referring to specific parts of the scenes.

- Ensure the language techniques are analysed fully.

The relationship between Prospero and Miranda is very important. Imagine you are directing this play and explain how you want the actors playing these characters to show their thoughts and emotions in these scenes.

`Level 6 (low)`

These scenes are where Prospero and Miranda's relationship changes for ever as he introduces her to Ferdinand and essentially arranges their marriage. The actor playing Prospero needs to show that this is what he wants for his daughter, 'It goes on, I see, As my soul prompts it', the word soul here shows us that this is what he really really wants for her and knows is best for her so the actor must ensure this is serious and not said with too much glee at his manipulation.

In the first set scene Miranda is torn between her duty to her father and the exciting promise of new life and wonder that Ferdinand offers. She must

really show both as she acts the scene; the love that she has for both but the sense of promise with Ferdinand, 'A thing divine'.

When Miranda is finally standing up to her father, 'O dear father! Make not too rash a trial of him, for He's gentle, and not fearful', this has got to be seen as a turning point and we need to see Miranda showing her desire to move from one love to the new. She doesn't stop even when called a foot and we need to see strength that we haven't seen before – after all, before she just sleeps when told to and listens to her father tell the same story again and again. This new strength should make her a more interesting character to act – she should even stand taller.

In the second set scene (Act 3, scene 1), we don't see Prospero and Miranda speaking to each other but she is thinking of him as she talks to Ferdinand and Prospero is watching her. The moment she tells Ferdinand her name she thinks of her father, 'O my father, I have broke your hest to say so!' and this shows us how she realises, as she moves from one love to another, even her father's commands can now be broken. Maybe this is the first time she has ever broken his commands – 'hest' – and so the actor could show her wonder at this.

Prospero is watching all this and his asides to the audience make us see that this whole love affair is a set up and essentially an arranged marriage, it's just that they don't know that. Prospero needs to show his glee at what is happening, even when the words he uses to describe his daughter are not very nice, 'Poor worm, thou art infected!' Calling her a worm and a foot really shows how arrogant he is and how he thinks he's better than everyone else, even his daughter.

The actors need to show in these scenes mixed emotions for both characters. For Miranda it is being torn from old to new love; for Prospero it is the difference in how he behaves to Miranda and Ferdinand and the asides he speaks to the audience.

This is level 6 because:

- It shows clear understanding of the characters and what they are going through.

- It uses some references clearly, choosing them to support and focus the answer.

- It provides some analysis of the language and how this tells us more about the characters.

To raise the level the student needs to:

- Ensure each quotation is analysed in terms of language and impact.

- Provide more analysis of the language of the plan, with specific focus on its effects.

page 188

Miranda's emotions change dramatically in this play. Imagine you are directing this play and explain how you want the actor playing Miranda to show her thoughts and emotions in these scenes.

`Level 6 (low)`

In these extracts Miranda goes from seeing her father as the only man in the world to loving Ferdinand and so her emotions change dramatically. The actor playing her needs to show this confusion and the pull of the different sorts of love she experiences.

The first key moment to examine is when Prospero directs her to look at Ferdinand and she is overwhelmed. The actor should really emphasise words such as 'spirit', which is repeated for emphasis, showing that she really can't understand who or what Ferdinand is. This is because she has only ever seen her father, Caliban and various spirits. The word 'spirit' allows for it to sound a bit 'other-world-ish' and so the actor should really emphasise this quality. When she goes on to call him 'divine' she should emphasise the alliterated 'n's of 'nothing natural I ever saw so noble' which will help the line to drive though and set the idea of nature against nobility. This links to ideas of status and honour and birth that are considered in the play.

Miranda's emotions take a real knock when her father turns against Ferdinand and she realises she has to choose between her filial and her romantic love. The actor needs to really grow in strength as she stands up to her father. We see her strength when she doesn't crumble but tells Ferdinand not to worry as Prospero is normally nicer than this.

In the second scene, Act 3, scene 1, we see that Miranda has really chosen her romantic love over her filial love and the actor needs to show firstly her uncertainty and secondly her excitement when Ferdinand also says he loves her. When she enters the scene she is concerned about Ferdinand and her language shows this, especially through the alliteration when she says the logs will weep when they burn, 'weep for having wearied you'. The alliterated 'w's draw the sound out and make it sound like crying.

She is a strong and determined woman and offers to take the logs herself but we see that Ferdinand would prefer to take the 'dishonour' himself. This is when she says that they are as noble as each other, which shows they are a good match.

The actor needs to show that Miranda is so excited and blown away by Ferdinand that she 'prattles' and this should be shown as excitement at her world having changed. By the end of the scene she is overwhelmed with happiness so has gone through all emotions but pulls herself together to leave Ferdinand for half an hour. Her language is complex and some of her words have double meanings such as 'I'll die your maid' because maid means virgin and servant, this needs to be pronounced with lots of emotion so the audience can see how determined and convinced she is in her new love and so we believe in it.

This is level 6 because:

- It shows a clear understanding of character and some of the language.

- It uses references clearly when it uses them, choosing them to support and focus on the answer.

- It provides some analysis of language techniques and effects.

To raise the level the student needs to:

- Ensure each idea is supported with a precisely selected quotation.

- Make sure the answer is balanced and doesn't fall into narration.

- Provide more analysis of the language of the play, with special focus on its effects.

Romeo and Juliet

page 177

1 1C, 2D, 3A, 4B

2

Quotation	Technique	Effect
'the bud bit with an envious worm'	alliteration of 'b'	Reflects the harsh and secret way the worm has infected the bud
'O brawling love, O loving hate'	oxymoron	Makes us really consider the qualities of these emotions – we see they are not as simple as we might assume
'What light through yonder window breaks? It is the east, and Juliet is the sun'	Metaphor – says she is the sun	Gives all the qualities of the sun to Juliet: life-giving, warm, light, overwhelming...
'love's light wings'	alliteration	Links these ideas together and makes them trip off the tongue as if they are light and bouncy
'Love goes toward love as schoolboys from their books'	Simile – love as schoolboys leaving their work	Uses a comparison we can all relate to – how eagerly students leave their studies – this is how eagerly love goes to love

page 179

How does Romeo change in these scenes?

Level 7 (low)

Romeo changes from a boy who is self-obsessed and melodramatic about love to someone who is truly in love. In the first extract he is just concerned with himself and talks about himself and how he feels. In the second extract he is focused on Juliet.

In the first extract we learn that Romeo has been moping around 'with tears augmenting the fresh morning's dew' and 'adding to clouds more clouds with his deep sighs'. Even before we meet him we know to expect someone who is really depressed and crying and sighing all the time.

When we meet him that's just what we get but we also see that he quite enjoys being so miserable and he almost relishes all the contradictions (oxymorons) he throws at Benvolio. Although he is miserable he can still do this word play. The oxymorons like 'loving hate' make us think about the fact that nothing is ever just one thing. This is like Friar Lawrence says later that no-one's just good or just evil. This idea goes all through the play because you can't just blame one person for what happened to Romeo and Juliet. I'd like to blame Tybalt and the Friar, but everyone did a little thing that added up to the big tragedy.

Anyway, when Romeo meets Juliet he changes because he sees that this is true love. He says she is

'the sun', which suggests that she is the centre of the world and all that is in the universe will rotate round her. This shows us that his focus has changed from himself to Juliet. This is one way he has changed.

He continues with the idea of the universe and calls her 'bright angel' which is actually moving the idea to the heavens. This suggests she is too good for the world. This might be a suggestion that she is going to die.

He likes using words again, but this time Juliet gets a few in and so it's more of a conversation and not just Romeo ranting on and on.

He changes finally because Juliet is stronger than he is and she is the one who proposes and won't let him swear or get the last word in their conversation.

This is level 7 because:

- It demonstrates an excellent personal knowledge of the text and the characters.

- It uses quotations effectively and provides some detailed analysis of their impact.

- It tries to focus on the question but sometimes goes off track.

To raise the level the student needs to:

- Keep the focus on the set question.

- Include a quotation as evidence for each idea, and develop into analysis of language and structure.

page 181

How is the theme of love explored in these scenes?

These scenes show us different types of love: childish, romanticised love (that Romeo has for Rosaline), and real love (that Romeo and Juliet have for each other, although it is still based on appearances). They also show the love parents can have for children and that friends can have for each other.

Romeo is basically being really self-indulgent when he is in love with Rosaline (it's like he is in love with the idea of being in love). He plays with words and makes it really mysterious to Benvolio (who is just trying to help him). He is so obsessed with Rosaline (or love) that he says 'this is not Romeo; he's some other where', suggesting the obsession has taken him over and changed him. (This sort of love isn't exactly positive then.)

Romeo describes love as 'a smoke made with the fume of sighs: being purged, a fire sparkling in lovers' eyes: being vexed, a sea nourished with loving tears' and this is shown to be true (he is the first and last one with Rosaline and the middle one with Juliet). This shows that love can be really different (depending on the people and how real the love is).

When Romeo falls in love with Juliet he realises that his love for Rosaline wasn't real and says 'He jests at scars that never felt a wound.' Showing that he can now feel the difference (so we are meant to believe in the love he now feels for Juliet as he's known fake love).

Rather than talking about himself all the time, Romeo now talks about Juliet and calls her a 'bright angel' suggesting he sees her as heavenly and divine (but this is a pretty normal comparison). He says she is 'the sun' and this implies everything revolves around her (including his life now). These are really big statements and show his love for Juliet and how it's bigger than his love for Rosaline.

Juliet's love for Romeo is on the same level (but she is more level-headed) and she thinks he's perfect, 'dear perfection' which shows she is also pretty head-over-heels. She's also more sensible than Romeo and worries about him being caught (she knows he will be killed, 'the place death'). She also doesn't want him to swear on the moon because it changes all the time: 'swear not by the moon, th' inconstant moon that monthly changes in her circled orb'. (This links with Romeo calling her the sun.)

Juliet uses language a bit like Romeo's and she says 'my bounty is as boundless as the sea, my love as

deep' and this links them (both talking about the sea). She is also more practical and she is the one who proposes to Romeo: 'if that thy bent of love be honourable, Thy purpose marriage, send me word tomorrow by one that I'll procure to come to thee, Where and what time thou wilt perform the rite'. (She's quite a modern girl really). This shows the idea that real love must end in marriage.

This is level 6 because:

- It has a clear focus on the question and returns to it throughout the answer.

- It shows a clear understanding of the presentation of love in the play.

- It uses quotations to support the ideas, usually successfully.

To raise the level the student needs to:

- Ensure each quotation is as short as possible.

- Provide analysis of language and its impact on our understanding and response.

- Avoid using brackets – the information is either needed or not.

How is the idea of deception explored in these scenes?

These scenes show that love can be deceptive and that people often practise self-deception. Romeo's parents know he's been crying in the sycamore grove but haven't done anything about it. This could suggest they've deceived themselves about the state he is in. Or it could mean they realise this sort of love is what every boy goes through at his age and therefore are just letting him deal with it.

Romeo goes on about his love for Rosaline and seems to be wallowing in it and enjoying the pain. He uses really flowery language and enjoys bamboozling Benvolio with his words and declarations about his love. His use of oxymorons is an example of how he enjoys language and uses it to befuddle Benvolio, another form of deception: 'feather of lead, bright smoke, cold fire, sick health' he uses so many it's really overwhelming. They create confusion and deception because they seem wrong but represent a world where not everything works or fits: a world of deception.

Romeo also talks about smoke and the darkness, traditional elements that represent deception and danger. When one of your senses isn't working you are more at risk of being deceived. He says that love is deceptive: 'love is a smoke made with the fume of sighs' and this reminds us he thinks he's in love and it's making him behave really strangely and it deceives him because he doesn't really love Rosaline. This also links with Cupid, who is meant to be blind, and Romeo talks about Cupid's arrow. He says 'he that is stricken blind cannot forget the precious treasure of his eyesight lost' and that says that she is his eyes, and without her he won't see anything. This is really romantic until we remember that this isn't true love, it's deceived love.

The balcony scene of Act 2, Scene 2 is set at night, a time that is traditionally a time of deception. Juliet uses the darkness as a shield so she can say what she wants 'bescreened in night'. This makes night into a shield but she was deceived as she could be seen and heard by Romeo. Romeo also thinks night is safe and he calls it 'night's cloak' but we know he's really in danger and might be killed.

Juliet talks about the 'mask of night' and this reminds us that they met at a masked ball and only really know each other in terms of appearance, and even that was masked most of the time. Their love seems really true, but I worry that they are also deceived as they don't really know each other. Romeo was deceived once before so he could be again.

This is level 6 because:

- It has a clear focus on the question and keeps it throughout the answer.

- It uses quotations to support the ideas and sometimes provides analysis of the language.

- It includes a personal response showing excellent understanding of the play.

To raise the level the student needs to:

- Provide more specific analysis of the language.

- Balance the answer so there is more on the second set scene.

- Make sure each idea makes sense and doesn't run out of control.

page 183

Romeo and Juliet both play with language. Explain how Shakespeare uses language to show they are a good match.

`Level 6 (low)`

Shakespeare shows us that Romeo and Juliet are a good match because their language is always at the same level of puns and twists and turns. This is true from when they meet at the party but we know about how Romeo speaks from when he is talking to Benvolio. They both like playing with language.

Romeo plays with language when he speaks to Benvolio with phrases such as 'not having that which, having, makes them short'. These word games are how he speaks to Juliet later at the party and you have to unpick his words to work out what he is saying. This play makes it seem like he enjoys being rejected in love.

He makes grand claims for his love: 'He that is stricken blind cannot forget The precious treasure of his eyesight lost'. This is his complicated way of telling us that Cupid is involved and that when you are in love you can't always see everything and that it is confusing and that she is like one of his senses, his sight.

Romeo tries to make these really big claims for Juliet; he says she is 'the sun' which suggests she is the centre of the universe and everything revolves round her. He uses lots of exclamations which show his heightened emotion and show us he is really emotional at this point. Then when Juliet starts speaking she also uses some and this links them. It shows they are on the same wavelength and this shows they are a good match.

They both categorise each other at really high levels: Romeo says Juliet is a 'bright angel' and Juliet says Romeo is 'dear perfection'. This shows they have a similar opinion of each other, which shows they match.

They both think that night is a good cloak or mask but it's not really, they are deceived in this. Juliet also knows that the moon is not to be trusted, and her language is a bit like Romeo's when he was talking to Benvolio because it is word play rather than saying straight what you mean. She uses lots of natural imagery like 'this bud of love' and this is full of hope for the future.

This is level 6 because:

- It provides a clear focus of the language used by Romeo and Juliet and how it links them.

- It uses quotations to support the ideas, generally providing evidence for the ideas.

- It refers to other parts of the play, showing good knowledge of the whole text.

To raise the level the student needs to:

- Provide more specific analysis of the language and the impact it has on meaning.

- Make sure each idea has a short quotation to support it, and that this is fully analysed.

Romeo's language is used to create his personality. Explain how Shakespeare does this.

Level 6 (high)

Romeo's language is full of extremes and wild comparisons and this creates his personality. He seems to fall in love really easily, and with Juliet it is passionate and fatal; the extravagant language matches his behaviour.

When Romeo is talking to Benvolio he claims that his unrequited love has made him lose himself: 'This is not Romeo: he's some other where'. He admits he is behaving out of character, but this self-awareness suggests he could do something about it but is being a bit self-indulgent. This creates the character of someone who enjoys being a bit dramatic.

The string of oxymorons continues and establishes this impression; it's as if he just goes totally over the top and gets carried away with the ideas. From 'brawling love' to 'still-waking sleep' he overwhelms us with his wit and these ideas really make us think. We get the impression of someone who really enjoys language and words and how they can show how the world can be a bit crazy. Normal language can't contain it, and this adds to our impression of Romeo's personality, maybe normal words wouldn't express him properly either.

He takes ideas such as being blind and develops and returns to them. This shows a determination and perhaps why he is able to take his own life at the end of the play – his personality seems to be that of someone who continues what he has started unless something happens such as Benvolio interrupting or a tragic event such as the fight.

All of these ideas are continued in the second set scene, perhaps to a slightly greater extent as he gets carried away and doesn't really listen to Juliet. She tells him not to swear and he immediately swears on the moon. This creates the impression of someone who is self-obsessed and also goes along with what he thinks he should say and convention – just like the unrequited love for Rosaline.

He uses really extreme language to describe Juliet: 'bright angel', which makes her seem otherworldly and better than what we have here. His use of alliteration helps to make his words really light and full of energy, 'love's light wings'. Here the alliterated 'l' creates lightness and this adds to our understanding of Romeo's personality because he is full of love and fun and youth.

This is level 6 because:

- It answers the question throughout.

- It shows thoughtful knowledge and understanding of Romeo's personality.

- It uses quotations and sometimes provides excellent exploration of their impact.

To raise the level the student needs to:

- Ensure each idea has a short quotation attached and that this is fully analysed.

- Consider planning so the answer is more balanced – some of these paragraphs seem to change idea in the middle.

- Include more on the impact of the language.

page 185

Romeo's emotions change dramatically in this play. Imagine you are directing this play and explain how you want the actor playing Romeo to show his thoughts and emotions in these scenes.

Level 7 (low)

Romeo starts the play depressed and revelling in his depression. The actor should really enjoy this melodrama and the playing with language – it should be a really good part to play as he really does go a bit over the top at times. In the second set scene, however, he needs to show the love is genuine this time, so it becomes a more difficult part to play as it must seem life-changing rather than fake again.

Romeo's first exchange with Benvolio is a great example of how he relishes the unrequited love that he is describing. He plays with his words, making Benvolio work to find out exactly what's wrong. The actor could play this with a bit of melodrama, almost making it funny as he is being a bit self-indulgent here.

This scene is also a great opportunity to show Romeo's extremes of emotions and the list of oxymorons should almost become a rant that tails off as he realises Benvolio is laughing at him. The actor could make Romeo laugh at himself here, showing that he isn't just this depressive moping over an unobtainable woman. This will help show the emotional state Romeo is in.

By the time we have the second set scene, the balcony scene, Romeo has been through every emotion and should be full of adrenalin and amazement at how his life has changed by meeting Juliet. He has forgotten about Roseline and mocks what he was, 'he jests at scars that never felt a wound'. The after-party atmosphere is totally changed into something magical when he sees the light and then Juliet. Now he becomes more difficult to play as he still has really emotional language with its heightened emotions, but the actor needs to make us believe in the love in a way that we didn't for the previous set scene.

One way to make the scene believable is to focus on the language. He makes grand claims, 'Juliet is the sun', and these can be played really dramatically or with wonder. I think the latter will be more effective as it gives us time to think about what this means and how he is saying that Juliet is the centre of the universe and everything goes round her.

Romeo's exclamations: 'It is my lady! – O, it is my love!' could be really unbelievable so once again have to be breathless and full of awe and wonder. They need to convey the idea that she really has captured his heart and he really is in love with her. The alliteration can help here.

When Romeo loses control and replies to Juliet, 'I take thee at thy word', we need to see this is because he is just bursting with love for her. The monosyllabic phrase means the words can just burst out of him like a machine gun firing. It needs to be passionate and full of energy and power. We also need to see that he really does mean it.

The old, expressive and expansive Romeo is back when he tells Juliet how he managed to get to her balcony. There should be no fear of the potential death that Juliet warns of as he's buzzing with energy and love. At the moment everything must seem possible and the language helps here. He tells her he got over the wall with 'love's light wings' and the alliteration adds a bounce that almost makes it seem like he flew over, especially when contrasted with the wall's 'stony limits'.

The Romeo we see in this part of the play believes that all is possible now he has found Juliet returns his love. The actor needs to play this carefully to ensure we believe the changing emotions and to ensure we believe this new love.

This is level 7 because:

- It has detailed understanding of the character and some of the language.

- It provides clear and detailed analysis of the character and how his behaviour changes.

- It has a clear focus on the question and keeps it throughout.

To raise the level the student needs to:

- Provide more short quotations so the answer does not risk become narrative.

- Ensure all quotations are analysed fully to explore impact.

- Provide more about the language.

page 188

What impression do you get of Romeo in these scenes?

Level 6 (high)

Before I read the play I thought Romeo was going to be a really romantic character, but in these scenes he's not at all, in fact he's rather self-obsessed and self-indulgent. He spends Act 1, scene 1 revelling in being in love and trying to demonstrate how in love he is, then he spends the balcony scene not really listening to Juliet, who has to do all the running and is the one who proposes! The impression I get is of a spoilt boy who is bored and has decided that love would be a fun game.

Before we even see him, we are told that Romeo has been 'With tears augmenting the fresh morning's dew' which prepares us to see a depressed young man. It is interesting that he is put into this natural setting of the forest and that dew and clouds are used as this links him to nature which suggests his actions are natural – maybe part of growing up?

When we meet Romeo we see that he is relishing the pain of unrequited love. If he was totally depressed he wouldn't want to talk about it, but he does, and at length. He doesn't care about Benvolio, he just talks about himself. The riddles he uses show that he is quick and clever, and are one trick Shakespeare uses to show that Romeo and Juliet are a good match because their language matches. However, poor Benvolio has no chance and isn't even given an opportunity to join in Romeo's showing-off when he reels off all the oxymorons. These contradictions are a bit like Romeo himself as they remind us that nothing is all one thing: 'heavy lightness, serious vanity'.

It is when Romeo is going on about 'Love is a smoke made with the fume of sighs... a fire sparkling in lovers' eyes' that I really get annoyed with him as I really get the impression that he is enjoying this unrequited love. He claims he lives 'dead' because Rosaline doesn't love him, which is totally over the top and gives me the impression he is just following the convention of loving the unobtainable woman that lots of poets at that time wrote about.

In the second scene it doesn't really get that much better. The only reason Romeo doesn't say so much is that he is matched (and maybe bettered) by Juliet who won't let him swear and actually proposes. He doesn't just talk about himself though, he describes Juliet as 'the sun' and this metaphor makes her the centre of the universe (that all the planets, like Romeo) rotate around. He's not as self-indulgent as at first, but he is still a bit annoying.

This is level 6 because:

- It tries to keep a clear focus on the question and provides a personal answer.

- It provides some quotations to support ideas, and some of these are analysed.

- It provides a strong personal response. This student clearly knows and has studied the play.

To raise the level the student needs to:

- Plan the answer more carefully so it is balance and has enough on the second scene.

- Provides analysis and explanation of the language and the impact this has.

- Avoid becoming too informal – the student is not chatting to the examiner!